I0459619

AN EXPENDABLE LIFE

Jerome Redd

Copyright © 2023 by Trient Press

All rights reserved. No part of this publication may be reproduced, distributed, or transmitted in any form or by any means, including photocopying, recording, or other electronic or mechanical methods, without the prior written permission of the publisher, except in the case of brief quotations embodied in critical reviews and certain other noncommercial uses permitted by copyright law. For permission requests, write to the publisher, addressed "Attention: Permissions Coordinator," at the address below.

Criminal copyright infringement, including infringement without monetary gain, is investigated by the FBI and is punishable by up to five years in federal prison and a fine of $250,000.

Except for the original story material written by the author, all songs, song titles, and lyrics mentioned in the novel An Expendable Life are the exclusive property of the respective artists, songwriters, and copyright holder.

Trient Press
3375 S Rainbow Blvd
#81710, SMB 13135
Las Vegas,NV 89180

Ordering Information:
Quantity sales. Special discounts are available on quantity purchases by corporations, associations, and others. For details, contact the publisher at the address above.
Orders by U.S. trade bookstores and wholesalers. Please contact Trient Press: Tel: (775) 996-3844; or visit www.trientpress.com.

Printed in the United States of America

Publisher's Cataloging-in-Publication data
Redd, Jerome
A title of a book :An Expendable Life
ISBN
Hard Cover   979-8-88990-084-9

Paper Back   979-8-88990-082-5

Ebook   979-8-88990-083-2

An Expendable Life |"Lord I Went, But Was I Sent?"

By Jerome Redd

Contents

SOMEBODY CALL THE AUTHORITIES, I GOT TRICKED

CHAPTER 17

THE REAL JOURNEY

Dedication

To Whom It May Concern

To my Muslim, Christian, Atheistic, Spiritual, or the just looking for the truth kind of person, every story in this book is true. Nothing has been embellished for the purpose of sales or profit. When I realized that I had not met anyone on this earth who had/has experienced what I have been fortunate to be such a part of to this spiritual degree, I knew that I had to put this into writing and share it with the rest of the world. And to my amazement while on this journey, I ran into another person who reminded me that I wasn't on this journey by myself. I just hope and pray that people don't judge it before they read about it. I hope that they can see the truth and the authenticity that took place on this spiritual journey of the lives which are involved. I ultimate hope that the person/s who reads this can and will find their own particular story within these stories, which will help them find and get closer to the person or thing which represents their form of God or God-head. My God and God-Head is Jesus Christ.

Preface

This book was initially written to celebrate and to demonstrate the awesome spiritual journey that I was fortunate to have with an amazing man of God. Nevertheless, by time I completed this manuscript, I believe that it was high-jacked by God Himself and is now servicing as an even greater purpose for all of those who get an opportunity to read it.

Notwithstanding, I have to also note that I believe that there is another high-jacking going on surrounding the things and issues as they pertain to God as well. And these apparent results, have left me speechless. As I listen to media outlets, TV, radio, internet, social media platforms and even while sitting in church, something is seriously wrong. Folks are just opening their mouths and stuff is just falling out. Notice, I said stuff? Some of it is so bad and so egregious that there is no identifiable label to even truly describe it. What is even more saddening to my heart is that this type of propaganda is prevalent today and is still growing. As a Believer/Follower of Christ, I would like to believe that I've been patient and considerate as it pertains to this matter. I was even hoping that the spiritual leaders of today would take a hold of this cancerous activity and perform the proper surgery necessary to cut it out. In addition, I also believe that so much of what is being disseminated in the name of God is in direct opposition to the written Word of God. But where is the voice of one crying in the wilderness saying, "Repent for the kingdom of God is at hand." I can barely hear a whisper. I also believe that this lack of accountability and refusal to confront the facts, has only made folks far more embolden and I believe as a result that the band-wagon has not only grown longer, but it has gotten even larger.

Recognition of a problem and the formulation of a strategy to eliminate that problem are two different issues. Since those that I believe should have taken the ball and run with it, haven't, I am then left with my own personal decision. What am I going to do? I could ignore the problem, deflecting the problem, glossing over the problem, or I won't resolve the problem either. I believe that I have clearly recognized that there is a problem. Unfortunately, I don't clearly have a solution to the problem. If I stand up in the arena of public opinion and voice my concerns based on what I know, I believe that it would be no better than just spitting into the wind while driving down the road. The outcome would not be pretty at all and when it was all said and done, I could end up becoming the bad guy. I then thought to myself that maybe the use of God's Word would really nip all of this in the butt and shut it down. I then also concluded, that these same people are misusing that very "Word" to deceive believers and non-believers. Uh-oh Houston, we have a problem?

To the everyday person or Christian, my proclamation might cause some trauma or at least some anxiety for them. Yet, the reason this doesn't cause trouble for me had/has everything to do with the life that I have been living, on an every-day basis, before man and with God. In addition, God also has allowed me to realize that this life-style was also the actual solution to the problem/s I seek. People can misquote, rewrite, and embellish ~~the~~ my story, but they can't change is the facts. What God had/has given to me personally for over forty-years of power-packed walking with Him, cannot be touched, moved or shaken by anything spoken or delivered, or lied on, by man. I also don't have to argue with what people say or do. All I have to do is show them what God has done, period. The choice is then, up to them.

Needing God, reaching God and receiving God can take you down a very slippery slope these days. And sometimes when you get to the bottom, you still aren't sure of the truth is or knowing whether or not you hit the mark. This book was not written to tell you whether or not you hit the mark. It is written to give you an example of two gentlemen that needed, reached and received what God had/has for them and planned for them as they walked this life. This journey about them is given to you freely and without bias so that you can see and know that if it is doable for them, then it is possible for you. It is not a blueprint for all mankind. It is only an example. It will give you a starting point, a middle range and even a rap-up. Each person, each individual on their journey has to find their own personal relationship with God. When you find it, when you've got it, nobody and I mean nobody can shake it or take it, period.

This book is not about proving the nay-sayer wrong. This book is about demonstrating that a personal relationship with God is doable and dependable. But you can't sit on the side-lines and wait for it to appear. By faith, you must take action and trust that God will respond. Too many of us have a great relationship with our friends, our families, with our Pastors, even with our Church. Yet, when it come to our relationship with GOD, we are in big trouble. Without the proper relationship with God, those other relationships will have problems. It is just a matter of time.

Please don't be expendable. Know in your heart of hearts that it is God Who has called you and it is God Who has sent you. The Bible says that if you know this, you will never fall. I hope that you enjoy reading this book as much as I enjoyed writing it. It was a lot of fun.

In our society today, there is a huge resurgence for inner-peace, collective-peace and spiritual-peace. Mankind is trying find himself; find each other and find God. Needless to say, we are having a collective trouble in the pursuit of all three of these areas.

We write books, we go to lecture and we attend church/synagogue/mosque. The reaching for this here quest, appears to be increasing, but mankind is not any closer to the answers. Since I reflect, represent and am I one of those persons in pursuit of these quest, I didn't have any of the answers either. But to my amazement and to my total surprise, I did find a way to obtain these missing and unanswered question/s.

In my overwhelming desire to get to know God on a deeply personal level, I ended up in a dual-relationship setting, which took me and a friend, into what I would call the stratosphere. Man, it was just out of this world. We enjoyed the places we had come from and also the places we had been taken too. Prior to this type of setting, every attempt made to fix or to figure it out, simply just didn't seem to work. Then one day, ~~we~~ he and I started a journey and God was with us on this journey. This manuscript is all about that journey. If you are one of those persons looking for the true and living God, I hope that you the reader will also take that journey as well.

The sharing of these collective journey's is both inspirational and powerfully. Surprisingly, they were not coordinated by either of the parties involved, when compiled. This book was initially written just to honor a friend. I just wanted to thank my friend. Yet, by taking on a life of its own, God's master planned was individually revealed and then manifested. These journeys demonstrate that obedience is far greater and more important than mere sacrifice. All you have to do is stick to God's plan. If you look real close between the lines, you will see that these two journeymen stay on the God given course provided to them and received blessing, after blessing, after blessing, and even some blessings that they didn't asked for or anticipated.

That's how God works.

Chapter One

Introduction

As some people read these stories, they might quickly conclude that it is basically about a Christian from Kenya, which meets up with a Christian from American, who in turn, compared notes and decided to stay friends for the rest of their lives. If in the absorption of this above spoken dialogue, all you can see is that, it is still a great and awesome story. But I hope that you will look beyond the everyday banter and see how these different episodes not only captures the everyday life of today's so-called spiritual men/Christians, but the real, the true, the ugly ups and downs of wearing that spiritual label and why it is even okay to doubt and even question the validity of whether or not, one is truly "Born

Again?" I hope that you will truly discover that it is okay to question whether you are listening to one's self, listening to the world or listening to God?

If I am going to be honest with the readers, I have to openly state that there was an internal wrestling that existed back then and still does exist today over my authentic Christian walk. There are times when I look into the mirror of life and begin the following dialogue. What is it that I want to do? What is it that I'm called to do? And what is it that I ultimately, do? This dichotomy, this cognitive-dissonance, at times, had/has me in a tail-spin. I didn't know if I was coming or going. This contradiction also forces and compels me to keep close accounts with God, period. If I am going to put it all out there and be truly honest with you, I can't even trust my own thought process sometimes. That sounds a little psychotic. But nevertheless, there is a positive side to this dilemma. God does not take away my liberty and freedom because I am now saved. Yet, I also know that above all, God knows what is best for me. I have also learned through trails and through my failures that I want what's best for me as well. Overtime, God and I have gotten real close when it comes to the decision-making processes for my life. I have discovered that I am now less and less disappointed with me, because I trust Him, more and more and more.

This book is not for the timid or the shy. It has something for everyone, but the question is, is everyone ready for what they are about to digest? I'm not expecting everyone who reads this to receive this. Nevertheless, this commentary is my truth. You don't have to receive it and you can feel free to even call me a liar. But what you can't do, is refute it and you can't prove it wrong. This presentation happened to me. This happened in my life. This happened to my friend's life and we aren't afraid or ashamed of what might arise in the minds of others, based on what they read within. This is truly an open book.

I've watched people, lived with people, known people and I'm still affiliated with some of those people who are living expendable lives and they don't have a clue of their very status or direction. And they are not bad people. There was a time when I was even one of those people. You don't have to destroy someone else's truth, to live in your own truth. What other people say and do should not be the determining factor of what and who you are. You should just be you. Your election, your calling, your happiness, should come from within. If it is not coming from within, you should look inside yourself and find that thing that really gives you joy and embrace it. Let your happiness, be your own unique happiness and not contingent on the views and opinions of others. I woke up one day and sadly realized that my life was expendable. I was not living my authentic true self. I was miserable. It was at this very moment that I realized that "I went, but I was not sent." I then got real sad and I then got real angry. You see, I also realized that it was I who allowed this to happen to me, freely. I had no one to blame, but myself. I then decided to do something about that. That is one of the reasons why I decided to write this particular book. My life is not expendable. My life is of value and I am going to take it and me back from where I have allowed it to go and I am not going to stop until I am satisfied that I've gotten it back from those whom I allowed to steal it. Hey! As you can well see, I am on a mission and I refuse to be stopped. So, what about you? What about your life? I hope that I can convey something to you and for you which will make a difference in your own personal quest?

The Story, Behind The Story:

I definitely want to take you on a journey, but I first want to give you a little background. I want you to see who the characters are, a little bit about their background and ultimately how their paths initially met one another. In addition, in the beginning becomes clear how important their relationship is with God and how this relationship becomes extremely important to each other. Yet at times, Jerome seems to dominate the commentary. Note: The only reason that there is more commentary on Jerome than Wilson in this story is due to fact that Jerome being the author and as well, the distance between the US and Kenya.

There is also a place and a position for you the reader to travel and explore as we take this journey into the unknown of our future of these two colleagues. You will find individual stories, collective stories and ~~just~~ even the unusual stories as well. Both Wilson and Jerome become your tour-guides of a sort as each story unfolds.

If you look a little closer or maybe at the end, you will notice something very interesting between Wilson and myself. Neither of us was truly ready for what was going to take place in our spiritual lives. By the time I had met Wilson, I felt pretty secure and stable as it pertained to my salvation and my relationship with God. It didn't take me long to realize that some of the strange things which were taking place that I had never seen or experienced before in my life and that Wilson was the catalyst as to why these things were happening to me. I also knew that in order to get more answers that it would require my active participation in the overall process. And that's what I believe really started this crazy journey and I wouldn't trade it for the world.

Background: Christian #1

Jerome Redd's Journey

I am a Christian, writing the story about some Christians, yet believing that the content of the story isn't just for Christians, but for all of mankind. I surmise that most people who believe in God or a God, believe it not because of what they know, but because of what they've been told. And if what someone has been told is wrong, inaccurate or false, then that person or persons are in a lot of trouble, period. Sadly, some of them don't even know that they are in trouble. And some of them spend a lifetime of not knowing this. Others wrestle with this deception of being deceived, while others die, never knowing that they were ever duped at all. What's even sadder is that in most cases, God gets blamed. And to make matters worse, the perpetrators/culprits keep right on pushing that same old lie/s and narative. I myself, was a victim of this very deception.

As a child growing up in Baltimore, Maryland. I was told that Christ was the answer to all of and any of my problems. I was also told that if I just believed in Him that he would solve/resolve everything going on wrong in my life. The only problem with this premise was that the people telling me this "Good News" weren' t living this "Good New" in their own lives. They talked the talked. But didn' t walk the walk. This in turn, left me with no basis of reality or stability. I was just compelled to take their word for it. And to make things worse, their actions contradicted their ultimate profession of faith. So, now I' m stuck. Whom and now what should I believe? Aside from this dilemma, I will have to admit that along this mysterious journey, that there was at least one, maybe two that did live up to those principles found in God' s Word about right living. They were the real deal. But since they were in the minority, their immediate influence had very little impact on me at that time. Now that I'm a little older, I am truly grateful to God for their consistency and impact on my young impressionable life, back then. And because there was at least one that was living it and giving it, and I got to noticed it. It ultimately, made a difference. Praise God!

I have run into a lot of religious leaders, pastors, Christians, Muslins, missionaries, striving for their best and trying to reach that spiritual realm that so many are hoping to obtain. A spiritual realm that not only connects them with God, but keeps them connected to God. I've also noticed that those in these leadership positions want this same type interaction/connection, for their followers of the faith as well. Notwithstanding, I've noticed that far too many of them have fallen way to short on this quest and many of them have ultimately, crashed and burned. I believe that their desires and zeal are commendable, but their ability to execute, leaves them at a huge disadvantage. Something is missing. They're either not where they ought to be or not where they've been called to be. There is a scripture in the Bible which addresses this, it reads as follows, "Give diligence to ensure that your election and calling are sure. If you do this, you will never fall." I have watched the fallen. I have seen the fallen. I have been the fallen. I can't speak for them, but I can speak for me. I fell short, because I didn't understand the true essence of this particular scripture. You have got to know your mission and your position. Without the necessary spiritual foundation, you will not know and you will not grow.

Let me explain. At age sixteen, I came face-to-face with my calling and election and I failed. Yet, I didn't discover this failure until another five years later when I was at my wits end, trying to figure out who was real and who to believe in.

Notwithstanding, I was one of the fortunate ones.' I was very blessed. Some people either never discover it or only come to realize it when it is far too late. As a direct result of this of this revelation, I not only discovered my true calling, but discovered that the essence and the difference didn't come from me, but it came from the One Who called me. I also learned that as long as I remembered and honored Whom was the true gift giver, I would always be in a position to grow and learn and move forward. Did I have all of the answers then? No. Do I have all of the answers now? No. But what I do know is where to go and to seek out those answers. That really makes a big difference.

So, I spend the first sixteen-years of my life not understand this concept of calling and election, while I was attending a/the so-called church, the whole time. Unfortunately, It took me another five years to recognize that what I thought I had previously learned about God and salvation, wasn't going to take me to or get me into heaven. I was headed to Hell. Yet, to my dismay, I thought I had resolved this salvation issue, some five years earlier. Please don't get me wrong. I am not ticked, but I am disappointed. See, everybody might not have sixteen years to figure this out or an additional five more years to figure this out either. They just might need to hear this truth; this story, now.

My ah-ha moment surrounding all of this came to me at Fort Stewart Georgia, in an empty weight room, while a thunder-storm was raging outside. I was going to five different churches at the same time, receiving five different so-called doctrines about how to be saved or become a Christian. But wasn't I a Christian at age sixteen? Yet, according to these guys, I had a few things missing. Now, here is the real dilemma? Who should I listen to or should I be listening to anyone of them at all? At that moment, I felt so lost, so defeated and so deceived. I didn't know who to believe and I didn't know who to trust.

Notwithstanding, in all of the inconsistency that was being toss around, there was one thing that did remain consistent, even back to when I was sixteen-years-old. That consistency was Christ. All of these churches and ministers, spoke of Christ as the Redeemer of all mankind. So instead of wrestling with the differences, I stuck with the consistency of Christ and move forward from there.

I took a bold step that day. I accepted Christ into my heart and asked Him for the forgiveness of my sins. I then put God on notice and made it clear to Him that I didn't know who to follow or who to believe as it pertained to the five churches I was attending. I told God that day that I expected Him to sort out the differences and to lead me into the right direction. If He was truly the God of Christ and the God of all mankind, then He could fix this as well. This day, I put God on notice. I challenged God and myself that I didn't want to play church anymore. I wanted to know Him for real, for real. I was directly questioning how was it possible for me to be so deceived these last five years? I wanted the real deal and I challenge God to give me the truth.

God answered ~~that~~ my prayer that day with a very simple comment, "Read My Word." I noticed immediately that things were not the same with me or with my spiritual surroundings. I also noticed that things weren't the same as it pertained to the Pastors of those five churches either. When I returned and had interaction with those five churches, I conveyed one basic response to anything that was said or given to me; show me in the Scriptures? And I repeated this over and over again. I eventually went from five churches to two churches. See, even at that young age, I believed that the Bible was God's Word and that He only allowed mankind to write it.

This declaration I made to God about sorting things out and putting stuff on the right track, had far greater implications than I could have ever imaged at that time. All I wanted was the truth.

Christ says in His Word, "I am the Way. I am the Truth. I am the Life. No man cometh to the Father, except by Me." So here I was asking for the truth, only to find out later that I really didn't know what I was actually asking for. God put some things in motion in my life which made sure that I knew right from wrong; That I knew the spiritual from the carnal; That I knew God's way, from man's way. I also, didn't see it coming. I found out later about the significance and power of that Entity called, the Holy Spirit. I learned that God affords this Spirit to every believer and that the Spirit guides you unto all truth. This Entity also clears up spiritual confusion, no matter who brings it or where it comes from. This revelation proved to be very important in my future walk and interaction with God and God's people and mankind.

At age twenty-two when all of this started making some sense to me. I was very happy and moving in a direction where God could really open my eyes to see where I truly had fallen short and the places that I needed to be built up. Here is what was truly so amazing. There is another scripture in the bible where God's says "That He will do exceedingly abundantly above all that you are able to ask or think." So, it just wasn't enough to get me on the right track and to focus me on my spiritual walk, God sent someone into my life, which I had no clue was coming, to show me some things that would truly blow my mind. I saw, observed, witnessed, participated and even engaged in nothing less than miracle working events that God wanted me to be a part of. I have never been the same and I will never be the same as a direct impact of these events in and on my life. Praise God.

For the Christian, the Bible teaches that God will not leave you comfortless. It also teaches that God places His Holy Spirit inside of the true believer and guides him unto all truth. And although I was/am a recipient of this awesome process, at the time of my salvation, I had no clue what this really meant or its significance back then. I now know that without this specific indwelling, I would have been involved in a whole lot more confusion and a lot more trouble. I would personally love to take credit for the amazing revelations that have been revealed over the years, but if I am going to be honest with others and myself, I have to give credit, where credit is due. The Spirit of God covered me time and time again. These are the real facts.

Christians talk a lot about this thing called faith and believing and acting on things that you can't see. I believe that my challenge to God about me not playing church anymore and this needing to be for real, for real in my life, it positioned God to do something very unique for me. God decided to send a man all the way from Nairobi Kenya, into my life and to change my life forever. This is exactly what Christ the Messiah did some two-thousand year ago, while on earth. His death, burial and resurrection, changed mankind forever. This man from Kenya didn't know that he was coming to America to change my life. He thought that he was only being obedient to the calling of God on his own life. At the time we met, we were both at different stages in our own personal and spiritual growth. Nevertheless, since we both decided to obey God, our lives would/have never been the same because of it. This man's name was/is Wilson Chiko.

Background: Christian #2

Wilson Chiko's Journey

In Kenya, Wilson was a pastor of his own church. He was spiritually active in his local community. He also ministered on a local Christian radio station. He had also established himself amongst other Christians locally. He was then given a full-ride scholarship to come to America to obtain a BA degree.

In addition, Wilson was also hoping that someone would continue to sponsor him for a Master's Degree program as well, when the time came. Wilson explained to me that in his country a BA degree is equivalent to a Masters and a Master is equivalent to a Ph.D. He told me that many a previous minister that had come to America in the past, had gotten their degree/s and promised to return to Kenya and preach the Gospel to the lost. Unfortunately, upon many of their returns, they made a lot of money from their lucrative American degrees, but never kept the promise of returning to preach the Gospel. Wilson, was determined and promised me that he was a man of his word and a man of God. He would return and he would preach the Gospel in his homeland. I had no reason to doubt that he would do just what he said he would do and he did.

Amongst his siblings, Wilson is the oldest. In his culture, this meant that he was responsible for the guidance and direction of the fellow siblings.

When decisions needed to be made concerning the tribe of brothers and sisters, everyone turned to Wilson for the next move. He was responsible for more than just his immediate marital family. He didn't take this role, lightly.

I also learned that when Wilson accepted this calling to come to America to acquire this degree, he was leaving behind in Kenya a wife and three teenage children. As the primary bread-winner for his family, this created a unique financial situation for this family both in Kenya and he here in America. Wilson response to this dilemma was to trust God. Wow!

Background: Two Men Of God

The Collective Journey-Wilson & Jerome:

Up until I met Wilson Chiko, I observed, I listened and I even at times, participated in the planting of the Gospel seeds for the Garden of Heaven, here on this earth. I willfully and eagerly tried to spread the Gospel as best I could. Yet, when it came time for my own harvest, there always seem to be some sort of lack. Yet, that was not the case or the example, with Wilson Chico's harvest. I saw harvest after harvest after planting and then I saw more harvest, in and around Wilson's life. What was God doing differently in Kenya or a man from Kenya that He was not doing here in my life, here in America? Nothing. I later found out that the answer was that God hadn't changed; but man had. The bible says that God is the same, yesterday, today and forever. Truer words were never spoken. That's why the steps of a righteous man are order by the Lord.

When I first met Wilson, I surmised that he was a strong Christian man of faith. But I had no clue of how deep his faith really was. I had no idea of his arduous journey, even up until the time we first met. Yet, as I watched incident after incident occur in this man's life, I begin to realize that Wilson was not just your average everyday Christian Believer. He had an anointing on his life, which left me in awe. He was more than just different. Well, at least that's how he appeared to me. I could not describe it then and I can't describe it now. But, what I will say is that it left me speechless.

When Wilson and I met for the first time at Fort Hood Texas, we unintendedly joined forces on this collective-Christian journey, because we were both compelled to get to know God better. This collaboration brought unbelievable benefits and insight into the hidden plan of God for our lives. We also had no clue, because we were both just trying to be obedient.

God is truly a mystery and mankind is always in the pursuit of trying to figure Him out. The Bible teaches us that when we submit ourselves to God, He gives us the strength that we need to not only change our lives, but to also become the men/person that God has call us to be. God can remove the mystery if He prefers. Yet, the amazing thing about this God and what He will do, goes to even another level. For the average person, the one-on-one with God is more than just enough and sufficient. But God doesn't stop there. God can and God will take that concept of one-on-one to a higher plane when His followers join forces. Here is what He says, " Where two are more are gathered in His name, there is He in the mist. " This is exactly what He did with Wilson and my journey of obedience. Wilson and I didn't initially come together to bring God into the mist. We ultimately came together because His Word says, "By this shall men know that you are my disciples, when you have love one for another. " All we wanted to do was help one another on our individual journey. Notwithstanding, it appears that the by-product of demonstrating openly God's loving fellowship is to call down the very presence of God in your midst. Every time we turned around the presence of God would appear. And another thing that God cannot do, is go back on His Word. I was constantly watching God just show-up over and over again. It was truly amazing.

I believe that each one of us and all of mankind is/are trying to figure out life and how to connect with the God source. Then the question becomes, how do I do that or how is that done? God and the God source can mean different things to different people. This can also pose a different method/means to reach Him. When it was my turn to pursue this journey of finding God, I relied on my only form of reference that I knew at the time. That reference happened to be the local church and the way I was raised in the local church. I also believe that others should be afforded their own way and means to find God as well. Even if that way or pursuit happens to be different from mine or even bad. There is a scripture in the Bible which states that "To subvert a man in his cause is an abomination to God." Let people find God the best way they know how too. The truth doesn't change because the method by which to reach God is different. The truth is still the truth. And God is still God. The Bible also says that if you rise-up early in morning seeking the Lord, you will find Him. The true/real God isn't hiding. If you really want Him, He will reveal Himself, period. I believe that God will draw His followers to Him in His way and not, my way.

Seeking God is one thing, but finding God is another thing. But if you really want to put the icing on the cake, you need to also obey God. Because Wilson and I obeyed the principles of God on this journey for some forty years, we got exposed to an experience that totally blew us away. Since we were unaware that it was part of the package, we couldn't prepare for it nor could we even articular what it was and how it was blessing us. We just received it, knew it was from God and said, "Thank you." This is also the same message we have conveyed and shared with others pertaining to this experience. Both Wilson and I are very blessed, but we are also very clueless as to what God had planned for us from the very start. But we ain't mad at God, either. It's called walking by faith.

I have chosen to share with you ~~in~~ throughout this manuscript, not to convince you of some of the stories that I have outline on how I came into my truth. But, I hope that as you read that you might be able to relate to my truth, in hopes that it may assist you in the quest for your own truth. The Bible teaches me that you can know the truth and the truth shall make you free. And whom the Son sets freed, is free indeed. Although God works with a collective church or gathering, I also believe that He has an individual program for each of His believers. But the real blessings show up, when we decide to do it on God's terms and not our terms. Before I decided to follow God, I did it my way, without success. So, I knew as a young Christian that God's way was better and I tried hard to do it God's way. My initial failures, proved to be very value lessons. I can only imagine that Wilson had very similar failures as well.

Wilson and I got to experience this awesome freedom and we are still experience it today. And we only have one explanation for this benefit. It is a direct result of obedience and faithfulness. In addition, these benefits are not reserved for just a few. They are available for all of those who love His appearing. Wilson and I are going to take you on a journey. We are going to take you on a personal and spiritual journey. We want you to come along on our journey and we want you to take notes as you go. We even want you to ask the hard question/s. If you chose to look real close, you will see that he and I were moving on nothing but blind faith, which God had to honor. And God opened door, after door, after door to prove to us that something out of the ordinary was truly going on. But His actions weren' t out of the normal. God took what appeared to be abnormal to us and made it appear normal. But Wilson and I were blown away time after time, after time. Wilson and I hope that as you read our stories that you get to see the same behind the scene God that we got to see. We hope that your faith will explode as our faith did. With no living examples for us at the time, we became God's living example/s and we are totally and miraculously humbled. I believe that God is always looking for and is seeking out, living Epistles to live and tell His true story. I/we hope you really enjoy what we have to say?

Background: The Reader's Journey

Mankind's desire to reach out to God and to connect with God, at the least, can be very confusing. In the midst of this confusion, humanity has come up with difference methods, ways and vehicles to expedite this feat, but mankind seems to always come up short.

I believe that this short-fall has more to do with us not checking with God first, versus checking with man. If you ask most people their opinion, they will give it freely in hopes that you will freely receive it. No homework, no research, no due-diligence, and yet where a person is going to ultimately spend eternity can be solely based on this given information alone. How sad. It can be solely based on someone else' s' opinion and their opinion only. This sounds crazy to me, but it is happening on a daily basis.

Am I trying to imply that the spiritual quest that you seek and the pursuit of it, does not lie within the activity that most men/churches are involved in? That answer would yes. But don' t worry, I got some more bad news for you. I personally, don' t have the answer either. So, the church doesn' t have it and neither do I. Sounds hopeless. Oh, but I do believe that I can point you into the right direction to locate it and obtain it. And not only to obtain it, but to be able to hold on to it for now and for the rest of eternity. That's right. I said it, because I'm living it every day.

Before I move forward, I need to ask you a question? Do I have your attention? If you answered in the affirmative, I need you to pay real close attention and put on your seatbelt. Because you are definitely going for a ride and it is going to get bumpy. If you answered in the negative, I pray that you keep reading and that you will eventually catch up. This book is not for everyone. I believe that it can and that it will be a blessing to all whom embrace it. But, if you have already made up your mind, I can't confuse you with the facts nor do I desire too.

I have learnt on my life's journey in the ~~pursue~~ pursuit of honesty and truth, truth always rises to the top. Truth will always outshine the dumb stuff. I believe that the bottom line is this "What are you going to do when the truth stares you straight in the eyes and you must make a decision?" And remember this, no decision, is a decision. But please, let it be your decision, period.

Now, back to those who answered in the affirmative. Is your mind opened to receive? Are you prepared to hear and do some things that you know are going to be uncomfortable? When you are ready to quit, will you still stay in the fight? Recheck that seat belt, one more time? Make sure that you pull it tight. Let's go!

Now that you have put the pieces in place to take your journey, I need you to do one other thing, first. I need to take you to and I need to guide you on, another journey. Once you have completed my guided-tour and you believe that you are ready to take your own personal journey, I believe you will do well and bowed well as you continue throughout life.

As I take you on this observational journey, please take out your mental and spiritual notebook/paper and take copious notes. You will come across some familiar examples and events that you can personally relate too. These events/examples are not placed there by accident or by chance. They are put there purposefully and for your confirmation. They will help you measure and determine where you are or are not spiritually and mentally. They will also help you in determining a step-by-step strategy for your own movement and growth, down the road.

Here is what that journey that I am going to take on looks like. I am going to share with you the stories of two young men, from opposite sides of the world. You will get to observe them and to dissect them on their personal quest to seek God and to also obey God. You get to see their ups and downs; their good times and bad; you get to see their successes and their failures. You get to observe them over a forty-year span of individual exerts as well as the crossing of each other's path on this journey. They didn't plan this. They were just looking for answers. I hope that their quest and the pursuit of truth, provides you with what you need and what you are looking for in your own quest.

This is their journey. It is not your journey. I hope that as you listen and observe their journey, you will find tools and concepts that will help and support your own personal journey. I have observed too many people today who are on a journey that has been created and development by someone other than themselves and God. This knowledge saddens me and is dangerous. If God isn't building the house, we labor in vain that build it. I believe that these two gentlemen allowed room for God to teach them and grow them into mature Christians and mature leader in their spiritual arena's. They let God build their house/temple. Instead of receiving the accolades for their gifts, they are always giving the glory back to God. They are confident that their strength comes from within, because it is God whom lies within. Another attribute is that they aren't sitting around waiting for someone or something to tell them what to do. They are always in the pursuit of ministering to the body and reaching out to the lost.

I hope that after you consume the stories of these two gentlemen that you will have your notes ready to start mapping out a blueprint of your own mental and spiritual journey moving forward. Their stories are not a blueprint for everyone, but only an example of what success can truly look like when it is surrendered to the Almighty. Once you have digested the contents of this manuscript, I hope that before you run on your own quest for truth that you might pass this on to someone else you know whom is looking for those same answers. Thank you.

NOTE: Meet Your Tour Guides

Below is a collection of stories about the life of two men on their particular journey to find true enlightenment. These stories are in no particular order, but they are written to provide a living example of the possibilities which can await you on your quest for truth. Here is their information:

1. **Jerome Redd**: Active Christian, Married, no kids, Born Baltimore, Maryland, lives in Baltimore, Md. Retired Army.

2. **Wilson Chiko**: Ordained Minister, Married, 3 kids, Born Mombasa, Kenya, now lives near Nairobi, Kenya, Professor at Day Star University Nairobi, Kenya.

3. Each chapter below will provide a particular experience/example on the journey. Yet, before and after each one, either Jerome, Wilson or both, will give a brief commentary statement. It is the desire that the reading focus more on the content of the actual story, than what it means to the character in the story itself. We wanted you to get more story than just commentary. Enjoy.

The Two Christian Men

WILSON CHIKO   JEROME REDD

Chapter Two

Setting The Stage

(Jerome's beginning) I was Robbed

JEROME got sold a bill of goods. His salvation was a complete fraud and he didn't know about this until 5-years later. Just read between the lines.

On my own personal journey of discovering "Salvation," I believe that the term/s "Born Again" "Saved" " Christian" " Accepting Christ" is and has been highly over-used and under-valued. Far too much focus/emphasis has been placed on the concept and not on the process. Too many people are running around talking about the name and the fame, but in fact, are putting Christ to shame. How do I know this? I am; I know; I was; one of those people.

Unfortunately, this misinformation/disinformation has lead a many a person astray and I was also, included in this mass confusion. How can I be assured of what I speak? Let me tell you a story of a sixteen-year-old young man listening to the Word of God being preached directly to him in his home church. For some reason that day, when the preacher spoke of the Gospel, I knew that I was lost and headed to Hell. I also knew that I didn' t want to go to Hell. To let it be told, the plan of Salvation was very simple. And the preacher told me exactly what I needed to do. So, I walked down that aisle and gave the preacher my hand and made a profession of faith publicly. Within a few weeks, I was water baptized and my fate was sealed. I am now a "Born-Again" Believer. NOT!

For the next five years of my life, I was under the diluted and misinformed concept that I was saved, sanctified and on my way to heaven. Nothing could have been further from the truth. In fact, I went through all the right steps and said all the right words and everything on the surface looked very good. But there was only one problem? My heart hadn't changed. The scriptures teach that when a heart has been changed, the old things are passed away, behold all things become new. The other sad thing is that I wasn't aware of at the time, was that I was lacking this critical knowledge about true Salvation. Nobody had sat me down and explained how this Salvation thing really worked. I can also believe that I was not the only person in this particular situation either.

So, when I departed my hometown at age nineteen to enter the United States Army, I thought that my spiritual status was in good standing. Yet, four years later as I am about to leave the Army, I realized that I was stuck in the mist of confusion from about five different churches on what was the real truth of God was and whether or not my Salvation was even valid. So, realizing that my so-called Salvation of the last five years was in question, ~~It~~ it was at this moment that I discovered that my true confusion wasn't with God, but with the representatives of God. This deficit ultimately balled down to who/whom I had been listening too. I now found myself between a rock and a hard place and it was now definitely, decision time.

So, I stepped away from those five so-called ministers of God and I spoke directly to God, Himself. No church, no pastor, no protocol. It was just me and God. I cried out for true Salvation and a means to get to know Him better. Here is what I spoke to God verbatim in my plea, "I remember how it was growing up in my church and we not going to play church any more. This has got to be for real for real." I also asked for forgiveness of my sins and asked Jesus to come into my heart. I knew internally that a transformation had taken place that day, because of what directly followed my profession of faith moving forward. I was no longer confused about who to listen too or what to listen too. When I spoke to anyone in and around the church and a/the question of what was true and what wasn't true came up, I just said, "Show me in the Book?" Most of these so-called men of God, could not show me. Their failure to biblically answer, only created more questions that they still couldn't answer. This only solidified to me that God made a difference and changed my life for real during this second exchanged. In addition, I had no desire to compete or be right about the outcome. There was peace within me, finally. Thank you, God.

It was at this moment that I learned that a true calling is based on a relationship, and not just a label. I also realized that true Salvation starts from within. I began to see everything differently from that point moving forward. I also realized that I wasn't the same person either. I knew that a real transformation had taken place within me and I couldn't find the adequate words to articulate what had truly taken place, but it felt good. Those five stolen years were now put to rest. God had truly changed my heart forever. Wow!

-JEROME: When Jerome approached God directly and not God's so-called representatives, Jerome found truth. Now, what was Jerome going to do with that truth?

Chapter Three

(For Jerome) God Went From Salvation To Confirmation

-JEROME: God doesn't just give you truth. He solidifies His truth. He explains His truth. He confirms His truth.

When I told God that I wasn't going to play church like I did when I was younger was my way of putting God on notice. I also believe that God wanted me to know that not only had He saved me, but He wanted me beyond a shadow of a doubt to know this in my inner-man what He had truly done ~~it~~ this time, period. He wanted me to have full and clear confirmation. Here are a few things which God did to reassure me of my conviction/s. I definitely stopped listening to all of those five difference preachers and then only attended two services, moving forward. I also started studying the Word of God and when speaking to church folks, I asked for the Word of God as it pertained to confirmation of spiritual matters and things they had to say. Don't give me your opinion. Give me God's Word. This shift in perspective made a big difference for me in my decision-making as I began to move forward from that point on. Then something very special happened to me right after I accepted Christ, which also solidified that this commitment was really real. The Director of the local theater group offered me a four-year scholarship to a college in Wisconsin if I would just major in theater. I was very good on the stage. I politely and graciously, turned down his request. I told him that I did want to go to college and I was flattered, but I had just accepted Jesus Christ as my Lord and Savior and I wanted to know and find out what this was really all about. I clearly understood that this could have been an opportunity of a lifetime. I also told him that I would love to be famous, but I believe that there will also be a day of judgement for all of mankind. This includes me as well as celebrities. I knew in my heart that I had to decline it, at this time. And although acting and entertainment opportunities have presented themselves over the years since, I've never regretted making that decision right after being saved to turn down that opportunity.

So, right after I got really got saved, I got out of the Army, got married and God sent me right back into the Army for another seventeen-years. Notwithstanding, I thought I was going to be a street preacher in Baltimore Maryland, but God confirmed that there was a bigger need for Salvation in the Army, instead of on the streets of Baltimore. It became apparent to me that my choice of decision-making was based and backed-up on the perspective of God's Word. I told God that I wanted to go where the biggest need was and at the time, the biggest need was in the Army. I would and I did listen to other people's opinions on this matter, but the final decision was always based on being God-centered and checking with God's Holy Spirit, first.

God first sent me to Fort Lewis Washington. Then He sent me to Korea on a hardship tour for a year, by myself. Then upon my return, He sent me to Fort Hood Texas. And although I had been stationed there once before while single, something interesting was about to take place there and I wasn't ready for. God was about to take my confirmation to a whole-nother level. I would come face-to-face with destiny and I would never be the same again.

On an educational level, I qualified for the Army GI-Bill, but I also qualified for the Army Tuition Assistance Program as well. One program paid 100% tuition for school, while the other pays only 90% tuition for school, while you were on active-duty. I choose the 90% tuition program and started taking part-time evening classes on the base. This allowed me to basically double-dip educationally. Once I retired, then I could use the 100% program as well.

And while I was eternally grateful for this gift, I was not the only person/s that God had also targeted for an educational blessing. There was this humble preacher from Kenya that He had also sent to Fort Hood Texas and it was by God's grace for our paths to definitely cross and intertwine and they did on this educational journey. I told you my background story of how I ended up at Fort Hood Texas. The story of Wilson is just as fascinating as mine, if not more. He ultimately, was just looking for an academic degree from America, which would afford him the ability to set Kenya and the world on fire for the Gospel. He definitely achieved that, but let me tell you a little bit about how Wilson Chiko and I first met. I think you will like it.

Wilson and Jerome's first encounter: We all look alike, right?

Both Wilson and I were working on acquiring at least a Bachelor's degree in Psychology and we happened to be taking a Junior-level Sociology class on the Fort Hood Texas campus. In this class, each student was required to do a report on one of the Family disorders outlined in the Sociology text-book. You then had to take this disorder and use the every day practical and medical examples of your own ideas and concepts that will work to solve or fix this given disorder. One of the Caucasian female students in our class, picked alcoholism as her topic to speak on. On the day of her presentation, she picked Wilson and I as her subjects to explain how to treat the disease of alcoholism. (She did not speak to either of us prior to the day or time of her presentation.) Her presentation didn't go so well. She assumed that both Wilson and I were from America and that we knew each other. Nothing could have been further from the truth. By the time Wilson had dismantle her entire hypothesis just for the people of Kenya, she was left speechless. Notwithstanding, it opened a completely wide door after class for Wilson and I to engage in a lengthy conversation about the nerve of people to assume that because our skin color was the same that we are and have the same background and geographical location. I quickly sense a bonding on our part and a closeness. Every day after that particular class there was moving forward of Wilson and I as good friends. We got closer and closer. We were always engaged in some type of dialogue. We also discovered very quickly that we were both Born-Again Believers in Christ. We then made it a point to take things to another level and we began to meet outside of class. It was at this time that I became blown away by the journey which brought this brother to the United

State of America in the first place and then crossed
my pathway.

Chapter Four

I Thought He Was Just A Preacher From Nairobi Kenya

A. Wilson's strange beginning: Stepping Out Against The Odds (Man said, "No way." God said, "All you had to do was ask.")

I quickly learnt that Wilson was not your average foreign student attending college here in America. I also learned that there were some particular struggles that had to be overcome to get both Wilson and his family here in the United States Of America.

Initially, in order for Wilson to complete this four-year degree here, he would have to leave his family behind in Kenya. You see, Wilson is married and has three teenaged kids. In the beginning, there was talk of possibly bringing his wife and kids with him, but that idea was quickly squashed once the issue of cost arose. Here is that heart-breaking story. Wilson is from Mombasa and his wife is from Tanzania. In order to get their family to America and be with him for four years, all of the townships between the two countries had to be paid a tribute, before they could travel out of the country. And neither Wilson nor anyone that he knew had that kind of money. Besides, even if he had the money to bring them to America, Wilson wouldn't have the kind of job or the money to take care of his family, while they were living here in this country. See, he can only work as a student on campus and in addition, he just might be able to make a few dollars preaching the Gospel on the side, but not enough money to raise three kids and a wife. Wilson was basically told to forget about his family coming to America if he still wanted to take advantage of this scholarship in

America. So, Wilson decided to leave his family in Kenya and came to America to be a student for at least four-years. That was a very hard decision, but his heart told him to go and Wilson did.

But this story ~~doesn' t~~ didn' t end after he left his family in Kenya and came to the US. There was an American missionary stationed in Kenya that heard about this plight and the Holy Spirit moved on her heart to act. She reached out to her mom in California to sell her car and send her the proceeds to her in Kenya. This White missionary took the wife and three kids of Wilson to every township that was needed and paid the tribute money and put them on a plane to the United States. What a miracle. What was supposed to be impossible, just became a reality.

Wilson was told to forget about his family and to focus on his education, but God didn' t. Wilson was told repeatedly that getting his family to America was impossible. And for those who told him this, they were right. But they didn' t check with God. That which was impossible with man, was possible with God. The next thing you know, Wilson had his family with him here in America. These are the kind of things which can happen and do happen, when you serve and on-time God.

If you think that bringing Wilson's family to America was a big miracle, please keep reading. Once his family arrived in America, he now needed the means and ability to take care of and provide for their daily, physical, medical and finance needs. Wilson, barely had enough resources and money to take care of himself. He had now been afforded the responsibility in a foreign land to not only take care of himself, but to take care of four more people and also go to school full-time. Wilson had no idea how he was going to take care of his family, but God did. And let me tell you, God did it ~~too~~ well.

B. God's Compassion: If You See A Man Destitute Of Daily Food… Jerome: "When we get paid, the man of God, gets paid."

When I first met Wilson, he was in his third year of college and was living with his family in Belton Texas on campus. When I first ~~met~~ encountered Wilson, he had no complaints. He was always praising and giving God thanks. Yet, I could tell that he was struggling financially to make ends meet from week to week. In addition, I also learned that his wife was having some medical problems and he had no medical insurance for his family or money for medicine. So, God had gotten his family to him in America ~~and has them with Wilson~~, but Wilson doesn' t make enough money to support this family. As for Alice and myself, we were both working full-time jobs, with no kids and basically, no bills. I was also going to college with 90% of my tuition paid, by the Army. ~~We~~ Alice and I were also praising and giving God thanks for all of His goodness. Yet, there was no way that we were going to sit on the sidelines of life and not try and at least do something to help out our brother in Christ, Wilson Chiko. I approached Alice, my wife and told her about their real plight. I also said that he is out there preaching the Gospel to Americans and that the Bible says that a laborer is worthy of his hire, as written in the Book. I stated to her, that every time we get paid, the man of God should get paid as well. Alice agreed. Alice and I got paid every two weeks. So, when we got paid, they got paid. And this is exactly what we did for more than a year. In addition, since we didn't have initially a local church we attended, we were looking for a venue to give 10% of our income too, anyway. This 10% is called the tithe in the scriptures. Giving this tithe was not an inconvenience. So, technically we weren't giving Wilson our money. We were giving him God's money. WOW!

This opportunity to be of service to a brother and sister in need, also brought our families a lot

closer together. Alice and Wilson's wife Rose, got
to be very very close friends. Alice would take her
to different places and also take her shopping. We
all started attending the same church in Temple Texas
as a family. We started a Friday night bible study at
my government quarter's and Wilson headed it up.
Some of the single soldiers from the base would stop
by from time to time, for the teachings and the
Gospel. I was in total disbelief of all that was
happening and taking place, because I had never
experienced anything like this before in my regular
life, let alone spiritual life. It appeared that
every time Wilson would step out on faith and trust
God, God would honor him and show Him that he was not
alone in any situation that was before him. I was
extremely impressed to see these miracles happening
on a daily basis in this man's life. And then God
decided that it was my turn. And guess what, I
didn't do so well?

-JEROME & WILSON: By this shall men know that you are my discipline when you show love, one for another.

C. God's Voice: "Jerome, Who In The Hell Do You Think You Are?"   (I wasn't trying to play God. I just didn't know.)

Everything between Wilson and I are going just fine or so I thought. There was growth, leadership, spiritual examples of God's great divine power and so on and so forth. But then an incident occurred that stopped me dead in my tracked and exposed me in such a way to make it clear to me that I had some unresolved issues that God needed to deal with in me. And God decided that He would use Wilson to reveal to me what those issues/shortcomings were ~~there~~. It went something like this. I received a phone call from a dear friend of mine back in Baltimore that she needed to borrow a $100. Since I had just gotten my check, paid some bills and made sure the Wilson had gotten some money, I didn't have a $100 on-hand. I told my friend in Baltimore to let me call around and see if I can find someone who could hook her up with this money, back home in Baltimore. Note, I have known this friend since college and she has never asked in the past prior to this day, for a dime. I was truly motivated to try and help my friend. I started making calls to one after another, after another, with no success. I was even getting a little discourage. I'm always helping others financially and now I can't get a $100. I then decided to go to my old faithful back-up plan, my mother. That's right, I'm a momma's boy and everybody knows that. When I called her for assistance, not only couldn't she help me, she claimed to have a gas and electric bill of $175 and they are about to cut off her lights. Excuse me? My attention immediately shifted from my good friend onto my mother. I continued to make phone calls, but still, to no avail. But now, my focus has shifted solely onto my mother's plight. In the meantime, I then received a call from Wilson. He was just reaching out to check on me and how I was doing. He had no idea what was going on in my life surrounding this money matter. I briefly mentioned to him about my friend and I was in the mist of calling folks for assistants in this matter and then found out about my mother's situation. He then asked is there~~is~~ anything he could do to help me financially. I told him no and as a matter of fact that he could help by praying over this situation, especially with my mom. After we got off the phone, Wilson definitely prayed about this situation. What I didn't know was that Wilson took it a step further. After getting off the phone, Wilson not only prayed, but also approached the church Deacons on my behalf and they took up a collection and gave Wilson the money, for me. In the meantime, I went back to making more calls after speaking with Wilson, but with no success. All of a sudden, I then get another call from Wilson. He stated that he's got the $175 dollars that mother needed, and it was at his house waiting for me to come and pick it up. I was at first, in total disbelief. I then asked him how did he acquired it. I then, declined his offer. And as I flatly refused his generosity, I also went on to scold him and tell him that I didn't tell him the story to go and get me some money, I just wanted him to know what was happening. I told him that he needed that money more than my mother and I'll pay her way. He apologized and said that if I wanted it that the money was at his house. I again told him, "No thank you." And I hung up the phone.

It was then and it was at this moment that I could clearly hear the voice of God's Holy Spirit saying to me, **"Who in the Hell do you think you are?"** And I **heard this more than once.** God has blessed you and God has prospered you on many levels. Because of your generosity to His man-servant who is preaching the Gospel, Wilson has greatly experienced the hand of the living God in his life. Now, that same man-servant has been given an opportunity to show to God his appreciation for all that you have done for him and his family and you refuse to receive his gift? **"Who in the Hell do you think you are?"** At this very moment, I begin to cry profusely and was so ashamed of myself. My refusal to accept his gift was paramount to blocking his blessing from God. Wow! This was the same as spitting in Wilson' s face. And although that was not my intent, that is exactly what I was doing.

At that very moment, Wilson lived about fifteen minutes from me on campus and I got in my car and drove to his domicile. I could barely see out ~~my~~ the window of my car while driving. I had trouble driving the entire way there, because I was crying the whole time. When I arrived at his home, I entered and asked him where was the money? I received it with thanksgiving and apologized for my poor behavior on the phone. Wilson and I didn' t have a conversation about this incident that day nor in the future. I immediately got into my car and drove back to my home.

It became very apparent to me that day that I knew how to give and to bless others, but I had a big problem when it came to receiving gifts, things or blessings from others. I still wrestle with this even today. But I am doing a much better job of receiving now, then back in the day. To this day, neither Wilson nor I have revisited what happened that day. I knew that there was an important lesson for me to learn and I believe that I learned it.

-JEROME: Blessings are God-made, not man-made. Be sure to check yourself, before you wreck yourself.

Chapter Five

The Spiritual Change Of A Lifetime

A. Abilene Vs Houston: Wilson; Acquiring A Master's Degree Or Listening To The Master?

It is now Wilson's senior year at his four-year college and he is about to graduate after these four-years with his Bachelor's degree. Since the Master's degree carries more weight that the Bachelor's degree, Wilson was compelled to weigh the odds. Should I stay or should I go back home to Kenya. With two more additional years ahead of him, there were also additional variables that Wilson had to also consider along with either staying or going.

a. The bottom-line was money. But there were also a few other factors involved.

b. Since staying and doing a Master's meant money for tuition, money to support his family, housing, etc. would be involved as well. Wilson, then returned to the original sponsors whom brought him to the States in the first place and pleaded that he felt lead by the Holy Spirit to go to Abilene, Texas and pursue his Master's and could they sponsor him again. This group informed Wilson that there were no resources available to send him to Abilene. Sorry.

c. While Wilson was telling me this sad story about there not being any money from his original source, he told me about another story that simply blew me away. There was a church in Houston, Texas that was aware of his situation and plight. They promised that if he came to Houston for his Master's at their Seminary that they would pay his complete tuition, housing, and moving for him and his family for free. I, immediately said to myself, what a blessing and a wind-fall from God to open up this fantastic door for Wilson so that he can get his desired Master's degree, with everything covered.

d. As Wilson shared this wonderful story with me, I was also totally taken back by the response he gave to this awesome invitation. He told the folks in Houston, thank you very much, but no thanks. The Holy Spirit is leading me to go to Abilene Texas. I didn't speak to or question Wilson's decision, but I was truly puzzled. Doesn't this generous offer resolve all of your physical problems and difficulties in this situation? It did resolve all of his problems, except one; The leading and the direction of the Holy Spirit.

e. After declining the offer made by the folks in Houston, Wilson packed up his family and car and they moved to Abilene Texas.

f. As I processed this story and considered all that God had done for Wilson up to this point, I just knew internally that God was going to open up a door in Abilene, like He had done in Houston and Wilson had nothing to worry about. Everything was going to be smooth sailing. Not!

-JEROME & WILSON: It's for the needy and not for the greedy.

-WILSON: The steps of a righteous man are ordered by the Lord.

-JEROME: I thought that He was going to provide all of your needs according to His riches in glory in Christ Jesus? Hello!

B. Jerome: I Would Have Gone To Houston and If it weren't for God, I would have missed my blessing.

a. When Wilson departed Central Texas, headed North to Abilene Texas, I knew he was not going to have the same opportunity there that he would have had in

Houston, but I knew that Wilson was trusting God and so was I. I also knew that the additional income, I was dropping off to Wilson every two weeks was going to be disrupted because of his new location. So about three months later, Alice and I decided to take a trip and go to visit Wilson in his new location of Abilene Texas. I also wasn't ready for what I was about to experience or hear on this visit. What Wilson told me then; still rocks me, even today.

b. As I sat at his kitchen table, he told me the following story:

-When they arrived at Abilene, they only had enough money to put a deposit on rent and on tuition; that was it. There was no extra money, period.

-Notwithstanding, his basement had standing water in it that he didn't have the money to have pumped out.

-He applied for a student job on campus as he did at his last school and there were no job available at this time.

-When he went to his Freshman Orientation, the professor told him and other preachers that there were no preaching opportunities in the local community, since all of their college professors were ordained ministers. (Note: Preaching locally was Wilson's main source of addition income, apart from Alice and I.)

-But wait a minute. Didn't God tell Wilson to go to Abilene? Yes, and he obeyed.

-The first Sunday that Wilson arrived in Abilene, he and his family joined the local church that his previous pastor had recommended him to attend. But Wilson did not reveal to the new Pastor who he was or that he was a minister. Wilson just joined and left.

-Every financial and employment opportunity that Wilson sought after was either closed or not available. But the Holy Spirit told him to go North to Abilene. How could this be possible? There must be some sort of mistake? There was a mistake, but it wasn't with God.

—Near the end of the first week there in Abilene, the Dean of the college, called Wilson into his office.

—As the Dean introduced himself, Wilson was concerned that maybe he was in some type of trouble of some sort. So, he asked the Dean was he in trouble? The Dean replied that he wasn' t in trouble, but that he needed to meet this, Wilson Chiko.

—He went on to explain to Wilson that in all of his years as a Chancellor that he had never received as many phone calls and inquiries about one student before now. People wanted to know how you were doing; did you need anything and was what could they do to help?

—Then the Dean asked Wilson was he okay and did he need anything.

—Wilson began to tell the Dean his story and what had happened since he had arrived in Abilene. The Dean told Wilson that he couldn' t promise him anything, but that he would get back with him later.

c. Then Wilson shared with me the following turn of events ~~with me~~:

-The Dean took care of the water problem in the basement. No charge.

-Not only did the Dean get him a job on campus, he got him the highest paying job on campus working in the Cantina, in the kitchen.

d. Then next Sunday, as Wilson was departing the local church with his family, the Pastor of the church put his hand on Wilson's shoulders and turned him around pointing to the pulpit and said to Wilson, "That's yours and my pulpit."

e. As I listened to how door, after door, after door was being opened and miracle after miracle was being performed on behalf of this man of God, I began to cry like a baby. This is impossible. This can't be true. How could God move in such a powerful and mighty way. I must have misunderstood Wilson's explanation of what had taken place. But I wasn't mistaken and I wasn't crying because of the powerful miracles performed and/or God's divine intervention. I was in tears because I knew in my heart Of hearts, I knew in my inner-man, I knew in my gut that I would have gone to Houston. I was so so ashamed that day and I called myself a Christian. If you are going to be honest about your relationship with God, some of you reading this would have gone to Houston as well.

f. Everything pointed to Houston. How could he have gone wrong by not going to Houston? Going to Houston was the only rationale and reasonable thing to do and yet, it would have been totally wrong. Call me Jonah. I would have gotten on the ship to Houston, hand's down.

g. This man Wilson Chiko, followed the Spirit of God and not the spiritual need. I knew because of his obedience in this matter that my life would never be the same. I made a proclamation that day before God. I told God that I know that I would have gone to Houston and that is not where You would have wanted me to go. I told God that day that I want the kind of faith that Wilson Chiko has, because I don't have that kind of faith in my life now. If I am going to be honest, there are a lot of Christians that don't have that kind of faith either.

h. Now that I am a little wiser and now that I am a little older, I believe that God used Wilson's faith to specifically show me what real faith is really like. God disrupted this man's life and family just for me. To this day, I am still shameful that it took that type of manifestation for me to truly see God in all of His magnificent glory through the environmental struggle of my dear friend, Wilson Chiko. Thank God and thank you Wilson Chiko.

     -WILSON: Wilson's faith was solidified.

     -JEROME: Jerome's faith was exposed and it wasn't pretty.

Chapter Six

I Hadn't Planned On Going To Kenya Or Have A Reunion With Wilson Chiko

-JEROME & WILSON: God is always working; sometime in the fore-ground and sometimes in the background, but He's always, working.

A. God ain't Finished: My limitations, Don't Stop God's Imagination.

I believe that the incident which occurred with me at Wilson's kitchen table in Abilene was just my wake-up call from God. There was more that He had in store for me, but I wasn't ready at that time to receive it. Yet, He did hit me right between the eyes and He definitely had my attention. I was in my thirties at this time. I had never heard of or met a spiritual man like Wilson Chiko, up to this point in my life. See, I had only heard about stories and people like this in the Bible. But wait one minute. Not only am I hearing and seeing about it, I have become part of the story. Internally, I kept saying to myself that this stuff happens to other people and not to me. It appears that God had already made up His mind and that it involved me as well. I would have liked and appreciated if He had just gotten my permission before He exposed me all of this stuff. I have to be honest. I was totally clueless. God had me at a disadvantage.

About ten years would past before I would get to see Wilson in person again. Our next encounter would take place in Nairobi Kenya at Day Star University. Wilson and I did stay in touch through written and verbal communication, once we both, departed Texas.

After Wilson got his Master's Degrees in Abilene, he returned to his homeland of Kenya with the main purpose of giving back to his people and preaching the Gospel. He was also involved in a few local ministries while a Professor at Day Star University in Kenya. What I didn't know was that things were a little rough for him and his family financially, but as always, God seems to step up and provide for him anyway.

After Texas, I ~~was~~ became an Army Recruiter for four-years and moved around logistically in the US for the United States Army. As a Personnel Sergeant, I was in high demand at this time. I was also growing and helping others to grow spiritually for God's heavenly army. When God decided to send Alice and I to Germany, I had no idea that God was going to use this deployment as a means for me to meet up with Wilson Chiko again. During this period of time, the Army was down-sizing, deactivating units and sending a lot of military families back to the US from overseas locations. I was involved heavily with these relocations for the United States Army at this time. In the meantime, Alice and I, moved more than most military families normally do in a regular tour to Germany. In the spiritual arena, Alice and I were regular attendees at a weekly Adult Bible Study on the local economy, which include Americans and Germans. We were leaders at the local chapel that was closing-down and it didn't have a Chaplain for our Protestant service. I volunteered and taught the High School Sunday School class for the teenagers of that base. I even conducted a lunch-time fellowship for co-workers of those in my unit that wanted a Bible Study. I also joined a youth group called Club Beyond as a mentor and chaperone for the kids. It was sponsored through the Youth For Christ organization volunteers, out of the US. I believe my active involvement was due more to the lack of people to choose from in the area. The Army was sending a lot of people back to the US. And volunteers were drying up.

It was through the group Club Beyond which got me to Nairobi, Kenya in the first place to hook up again with Wilson again. This program was/is throughout the states and overseas. It is set up as an out-reach to mentor and reach young people for Christ. We would meet once a week locally and then had local trips and as well distance trips, which impacted these kid's lives. There are no words to describe how it feels or touches you when one of those young people makes a personal profession of faith. You get to spend really quality of time with these young people. I watched and got to work with this one woman from Virginia (Cindy) and she really had a way with those kids and the kids loved her as well.

Then Club Beyond was planning a missionary outreach trip to Nairobi, Kenya, from Germany and they were looking for volunteers who could get off from work and attend it. They were looking for students, teachers and chaperones to help build a playground from scratch at a local school there. This trip was going to take about three weeks. Knowing that my friend Wilson was working at the Day-Star University in Nairobi and living nearby, I was highly motivated to attend this missionary trip. I also just wanted to make a difference. So, I volunteered. But was this what God wanted for me/you to do? Now that is the real question?

Questions, questions, questions: If I am going with Club Beyond on this trip, how am I going to meet up with Wilson in Nairobi? How close or how far is Wilson from where I am going to be? If Wilson and I can communicate once I arrive, it is possible for us to meet, in country? I knew that I had some money for Wilson's ministry, but would I be able to get it to Wilson? Above all, I knew that I had more questions than answers and the prospect of hooking up with Wilson, didn't look promising at all. But, if I am going to be honest, I have to admit that my perspective was based on Jerome's insight and not God's ability. What then? There were a lot of if's, but I serve a Mighty God that deal with the if's and the impossible. Besides, I had nowhere else or no one else to turn too, but God.

In retrospect, it dawned on me that instead of looking and focusing on the possibilities, I was focusing on the impossibilities. Getting to Nairobi to help build a playground for under-privileged kids, along with supervising kids to help others and get some money to my spiritual brother, was completely out of my control. The only way to make this happen was to let go and to let God. There is a scripture in God's Word which says, "If this be of man it shall come to naught. But if this be of God, no man can stop it." It was at this moment that I could stop, relax and watch God do some amazing things as I took this trip to another country. I also had no clue what God had in store for me as this experience was to unfold. As a matter of a fact, the very first day that I arrived in Nairobi, God made sure that I knew beyond a shadow of a doubt that He had orchestrated and put in place a series of events and experiences that were going to change, impact and touch, multiple lives. Below are just a few of those miraculous experiences. Enjoy.

-JEROME & WILSON: When all else fails, God can and God will.

Chapter Seven

The Kenyan Connection

The love of God is universal.

Ten-years earlier when Wilson stepped on to the shores of the United States, God truly revealed and demonstrated to Wilson that His powers were not just restricted to the country of Kenya. I became part of this revelation and documented witness on behalf of Wilson. I was humbled and considered it a privilege that God would use me in this capacity. What I was totally unaware of was that now it was my turn. Wilson came to America and God showed off. Now I am headed to Kenya and for the next three weeks, I am going to get a ~~chase~~ chance to see God show off for me. And believe me folks, God put on a show.

-JEROME: Was I ever in any real danger? I don't think so.

1. The Kids Of Kenya Are Different Than The Kids Of America, Right? Not!

a. When I arrived in Nairobi, my first day was extremely interesting to say the lease. Since our group of volunteers collectively were not going to be in the local town again until we left to go back home, they gave everyone in our group an opportunity to sight-see for about two hours, in the local township. After our sight-seeing, we would then head out to a place called, Camp Womba. This is where we would be staying each night for most our time while we were here. It was a fenced-in wooded area, surrounded by plenty of wild animals.

b. As an African-American in my homeland of Kenya, I was extremely curious as it pertained to my surroundings and the people of Africa. I initially visited some of the shops, but I didn't purchase anything. I also traveled through the streets of this town and watched both the natives and the tourist as they interacted.

c. As I walked down one street, I noticed to my right, a group of young boys off to the side of the road. I would say that there were about 8 of them and they ranged in age from about 8-14 years old. Because I worked with Club Beyond and its young people, I was extremely curious about these young men and who they were. There were no females in the group. Yet, something compelled me to reach out and have a conversation. As we began to engage, it appeared that they were as curious about me as I was about them. I was totally fascinated. And there was this particular young man that stood out from the crowd. His name was Abraham.

d. I could quickly assess that Abraham was the leader or at least, one of the leaders. My instinct told me that this might be a good opportunity to learn more about the culture of Kenya and the local people. So, I asked the entire group the following inquiry. Isn't today a school day? They all replied to me in the affirmative. I then said, "If that is so, why are you boys, not in school?" I first heard a little chuckle from the boys and then Abraham said, "School cost money and our parents can't afford to send us to school." Then I replied with the following. "Seeing that you guys don't have money for school, but you instead are out here hanging on the streets, yes?" I then got a big smile from most of the kids. I then made a profound statement that was not lost on anyone that was present. I then said the following, "I don't know how things are here in Kenya, but in America, when young boys don't have something productive to do, they tend to get into trouble." This response brought laughter from all the boys. I also felt that their laughter opened the door for further dialogue. This made it perfectly clear to me that there was no difference in kids from Kenya and the rest of the world. I was totally blown away. I also believe that this exchange, brought about a positive connection between these boys and myself. Some might even say that this connection probably kept me from getting robbed and/or hurt. These kids were open and honest with me and they didn't even know who I was. I believe that God had already gone before me and had prepared their hearts to receive me.

e. I also believe that the Spirit of God compelled me and prepared my heart to have compassion on these boys in this given situation. I then called out Abraham to the side, and with my back to the other boys, I pulled out some Kenyan money and also some American money and gave it to Abraham. I told him that he knew who needed what the most and who didn't. I also told him that I believed that he would do the right thing by those other boys and share this money with them. I then walked away feeling extremely good and generous. I later caught up with the rest of the volunteers and we got back on the bus and headed to Camp Womba for the evening.

f. There is something very interesting and strange about this first encounter. When I arrived at the camp that night, you can only image the story that I had to tell others about my personal trip to the local village. I first shared it with the volunteers who came with me from Germany and then the folks at the camp about my encounter with Abraham and the boys. I also later shared this same story with some of the folks who lived at the camp on a daily basis. These folks that live at the camp daily, were in shock as I shared this story about the boys. They looked at me with disbelief. They couldn't believe that this had happened and that I had been able to walk away unscathed and unmolested. I then queried them about their grave concerns. They stated to me countless times where outside visitors and their visitors encountered group of young men like these that and were then beaten-up or rob or both. I then heard someone say to me that you were lucky. I said no, "I'm blessed." I had no idea, how much danger I was in, but it didn't matter at the time, because I knew in my heart that God was present when I met those boys. And God was being reflected to those boys and they had no other choice but to honor God, not me. Amen. I would like to believe that I was the first or one of the first African-American men that those young boys had met. When they met me, they weren't looking for money, they were looking for information. Once they had obtained what they were looking for, they had no reason to rob or hurt me. That is why they let me go after the encounter. Notwithstanding, I also got to meet up with Abraham again, just before I departed Kenya. I don't believe that it was just an accident that day when we met. God had decided that Abraham and I, would meet, again.

-JEROME: Pay attention. Pay attention.

2. Being Broke-Down, Can Lead To A Break-Through

a. After we build the playground for the school, we were all scheduled to go on a Safari. Since this was my first Safari, I like many others were completely blown away by the travel, the animals and the treatment. I was very excited about the entire process and not just the seeing of the animals. We were all briefed before we departed so that we could all have an enjoyable and safe trip. When we traveled, we went in a convoy of three vans, to and from our destination. Everything was first class and there were no hiccups during the Safari itself. Yet, on our way back to the camp, one of our vehicles, broke down. All three vehicles pulled to the side of the road and all three drivers attempted to assess/assist with the problem. The town we stopped in consisted of two buildings. One building on opposite sides of the street. That was it. That represented a town.

b. All of the drivers went to and worked on the van that was having the problem. The drivers encouraged us to go into the store and do some shopping while they tried to fix the broke down van. Seeing that we were in tourist mode, I believe that most of us figured that it might take them about thirty minutes or so and we would be back on our way. I believe that God had some other plans for this occasion and I strategically watched it unfold.

c. As tourist, we noticed that it was extremely hot. There was no shade anywhere and it appeared to be getting even hotter in the sun. As we sat around, after shopping, the discomfort started building up. People were complaining about the heat, the van being broken down and how inconvenient all this was on us. Then one of the strong brother's in Christ spoke the following: "Why are we complaining about the inconvenience of this situation, instead of looking at this as an opportunity to witness." The prophetic words he spoke, pierced my heart and prompted me into action.

d. I then began to give my testimony to those in our small group and others who were listening. I also noticed that some of the others that were listening were outsiders and locals, from Kenya. It appeared that the more I spoke, the bigger the crowd got. So, I spoke some more. Next thing you know, most of all of those that were around me were from Kenya and not with us. I was fired up and I couldn' t be stopped.

e. I then got on the topic of the importance of God' s Word and obeying God' s Word alone. I started talking about the Bible being God' s final authority and not even what I had to say was good enough if it didn' t match up to the infallible, Word of God. One of the young men listening, proceeded to asked me for a Bible.

f. Interestingly enough, I had taken a smaller version of my Bible with me on the Safari and I had about 4 or 5 pockets sides Bibles in my back pack on the van. I then went to retrieve the bibles. When I returned from my van, I gave the man who asked for a Bible, a Bible. Yet, to my amazement, others wanted a Bibles as well. I gave away all four of the extras that I had and I told the rest of them that I'm sorry, I gave away all that I had and the one that I have left, is mine. One of the ladies in the store heard about the Bible being given away and came out and asked me for one. I told her that they were all gone. She broke down in tears. I was overwhelmed. The hunger to have their own individual bible, caught me off guard. I did get her address and sent her a bible after returning to Germany. As all of this was unfolding, I was amazed and asking God the question. What just happened? What is going on? I had no idea how valuable the Bible/s were to these folks until this happened.

g. This incident shook me and also left me puzzled. At that moment, I knew in my heart that I was more concerned about being a tourist than I was about preaching the Gospel. It took someone from our group who was more focused and an engaged in his relationship with God to get me provoked. Afterward, I then open my mouth and shared the Good News. I almost missed an amazing opportunity to represent God. The second thing that got me about all of this was their hunger for ~~the~~ God's Word or at least to have it in their possession. They treated that Bible as if it were pure gold. We American's take our access to having the Bible at our disposal, for granted. Not these people. They reverenced and eagerly pursued God's Word. Wow!

h. How could a trip on a Safari, turn into a soul-searching and heart-wrenching experience about watching as well as praying for me, lest we enter into temptation? It appears that that little break-down, turned into a powerful break-through, at least for me. I tell you, this is what can happen when God steps in.

-JEROME: When I saw the real Jerome in the mirror, I didn't like what I saw.

3. Which Gospel Will You Preach? I Thought I Was Ready

a.   I was also very fortunate to participate in some other activities that just blew me away as well. Because I was an African-American male in Kenya, I was considered by the natives, unique in stature. Those at our camp, hooked up a meeting for me to meet with one of the local Maasai Tribes. I got to meet with the tribal leader and his followers. Someone from the camp was the translator. They asked me some questions and I asked them some questions. This was the first time that they were meeting with an African-American. It was an awesome and amazing experience.

b. Another fantastic adventure occurred when we were ask did we want to visit a traditional Kenya village and observe a Kenyan wedding ceremony. While in route to that village, one of our vehicles had a flat tire. I discovered that the flat was due to a Cassia needle, which comes from a Cassia tree. These needles are very long and can go right through tires and tennis shoes. We immediately changed the flat with a spare tire, but we needed to get the flat fixed also. These needles are everywhere. There is always the concern about possibly getting another flat, so you had to have the spare fix as soon as possible also ~~as well~~. When they dropped everyone off from our group at the village, the driver asked did anyone want to go in town with the driver to assist in getting the flat tire fixed. Another Christian brother and myself volunteered to go into town with him. What happened next, just blew me away.

c. After getting the flat fixed, we returned to the village where the ceremony was being held. Everyone before us had already been taken through the huts and had witnessed the mock wedding ceremony, while we were in town. Because we volunteered to help, we got and individual tour, verses a group tour. As we enter the village, the first thing I noticed upon my arrival was the smell. They use manure on the grounds and on the huts. It has a very interesting smell and it definitely attract flies. Secondly, as we enter the one hut, the guide was pointing out the sleeping quarters for the husband, the wife, the goat and maybe even a baby if they have one. What truly took me back was the mock bride who was sitting on the bed, waiting for the wedding ceremony to begin and she was completely still and she was completely alive.

d. I cannot and will not ever forget that day for the rest of my life, what I observed. As I saw this woman sitting on the edge of this bed, waiting for the wedding ceremony to begin, I noticed just how still she was as she sat there, but I could occasionally, see her eyes move. I also noticed because of the manure that there were a lot of flies around and in the hut as well. She even had at least two to three flies at any one time, crawling on her face. Yet, she did not move. While in the hut, as I observed her and watched her, I was constantly swatting away the flies off of my own person; let alone my face. Yet this woman portrayed her role without even flinching. That evening when I returned to the camp, I could not get the image of this woman out of my head. This particular incident, shook me to my very core; to my very being. As a Christian, I am called and compelled to preach and teach the Gospel of the Good News of Christ. I am called to do this all over all the world, including Nairobi Kenya. What if God sent me to Kenya to preach the Gospel? Would I have the same self-disciple as this young Kenyan woman to accomplish this task? I don't think so. If I spent as much time swatting the flies as preaching the Gospel to people, who would even listen to the words I speak? They would be so distracted by my swatting movements that they would not be listening to what I would have to say about saving their souls. Houston, we have a problem.

e. After I wrestled and wrestled with this internal dilemma and as well as my thoughts about the van that broke down as we returned from the safari, I had to do a deep reality check. I had to do one of those, gut check's. I was compelled to internally question what I had spoken all these previous years about being a true witness for Christ. Can Christ really depend on me? My mantle was looking a bit shaky if you asked me. After this encounter, the only thing that I was assure of was that I could talk a good game. I knew how to make me sound good and make people believe that I was who I said I was. Yet now, I'm not so sure. This chain of events not only shook me, I wanted to reach out and have a conversation with someone about what I was personally and spiritually going through. Yet, considering the overall limitations surrounding this entire episode, I did the next best thing for me. I then went and wrote the following poem about it. It's called: "Which Gospel Will You Preach?" It gave me what I needed to continue to fight the good fight of faith.

It also truly humbled me like I had never been humbled before. (See below)

WHICH GOSPEL WILL YOU PREACH?

Take out some time, to know yourself.

Review all those things, you've known and felt.

Look real hard and look real deep.

Don't overlook, even the smallest of peeps.

See the time will come, when you must say.

If not now, no doubt, some day.

How much does the Gospel, mean to you?

How far will you go, just to see it through.

Will you leave your house, will you leave your land?

Will you leave the things you know and understand?

What about your soft bed, and your spouse nearby?

That super bowl game, my suit and tie.

See, a comfortable Gospel, is so ideal.

It's very convenient, but it's also, unreal.

We unwittingly put, restrictions on God.

Serving Him with our lips, and finding something's, too hard.

If we'll search deep and hard, and give Him our heart.

Be honest with Him, from end and the start.

Putting all on the alter, with nothing to hide.

Let the Jesus come out, that's on the inside.

Then I will know, what I have to do.

Not concerned about Martha, or John or you.

Just go where the Spirit, has already prepared.

The US, maybe Kenya or just anywhere.

So, I ask myself again, as I put these words down.

Will it be the true Gospel or the just here and now?

I know men are dying, they're dying in sin.

Someone must go forth, so that others can win.

So, as God sends out the call, to the lost and the free.

I want to be able to say, here am I Lord, here am I Lord, here am I Lord, send me.

Jerome Redd, April 15, 1995

-JEROME: Pay attention, so you can see the real miracle.

4.   A Few Fishes And Just A Loafs Of Bread

a.   I mentioned earlier how when I arrived in Nairobi on the first day that something amazing happened ~~with~~ between me and some young Kenyan street boys. One of those boy's names was Abraham. As I got to know the local people at the camp that we stayed at, I became very close to young missionary man named William. I could tell that he was sincere and had a good soul. He and I had lot of conversations together about life, the Word of God and Salvation. On the day that I was scheduled to go to town to meet with my friend Wilson Chiko, William came along into town with me to help get supplies and to drop me off at Day-Star University to meet with Wilson.

b.   William was very successful with the accomplishment of this mixture of missions and me. He dropped me off at Day Star, picked up supplies and

then returned to pick me up and return us to Camp
Womba. After picking me up from my Day-Star visit
with Wilson, William decided to stop in the local
village so that I could get something to eat for
lunch. I hadn't eaten since earlier that morning and
it was now after lunch. In spite of all of the
excitement that had taken place on this local trip
for me, I felt compelled to share with William about
the story of meeting the Kenyan boys on my first day
to this country. I knew that sharing this information
would be important to William. He made it clear that
one of his callings was to reach those young lost men
whom had been target and over-looked by society, in
his country.

c. Then out of nowhere as William and I were
walking to the store, I run into Abraham again. And I
believe that this was no accident. I then introduce
~~him~~ Abraham to William for the first time. After our
greeting, I asked Abraham how was he doing and did he
need anything? Abraham stated that he was fine, but

he was hungry. Note, when I met Abraham at this moment, there were only 2 or 3 other boys with him at that time. When he said that he was hungry, I said to Abraham to wait here. I immediately walked into the nearby store where we had just passed and purchased a couple packs of bologna and a loaf of bread. I did not immediately exit the store. I stayed in the store and made sandwiches for Abraham and his crew. To my amazement, when I existed the store, there weren' t just three boys, there was about 20 boys waiting for me. I didn' t have 20 sandwiches. I only had about 15/16 sandwiches for consumption.

d. When I approached the group with the bag full of sandwiches, I told Abraham that he knew who was the most deserving and the most needful. So, based on Abraham' s approval, he would determine who received a sandwich or not. When I got to the last sandwich, I gave it to Abraham. I didn' t even get a sandwich for myself. Immediately after all of the sandwiches were given out, everyone dispersed. Both William and I were left abandoned, just as quickly as we were surrounded. It was a site to behold.

e. Not wanting to lose the significance of this precious moment, I then turned to William and asked him, did he realized what just happened in this ~~matter~~ encounter? His initial response gave me the impression that he appeared to have missed it. But I in-turn, chose to enlighten him. I explained to William that these young men of Kenya appear to get the same bad rap as the young men of America get, due to their misfortune and poverty. Nevertheless, these kids didn' t get a bad rap from me, the visitor from America. That visitor from America ~~that~~ looks just like them. Notwithstanding, they got just the opposite. They got a good report from me. They also got some money from me without having to attack me or to hurt me. Then after I meet them a 2nd time, I still have/had something good/positive to say and pass on to them. I also gave them something to eat for their bodies. This is a good thing. Now, you as a missionary from Kenya, these are the same type of young men that you are trying to reach with the Gospel. Think about this, those young men appreciate what I have done once, on their behalf and on the 2nd time I did something nice for them also, and you just happened to be there with me, when it happened on the 2nd time. I'm going back to the US tomorrow. Now when you come back to town to witness to them, they'll remember that you were the Kenyan that was with the American, which was so kind to them. If they are willing to receive my money and my physical food, maybe they will also be willing to receive your spiritual food that you have to offer them as well. I then saw a smile come over William's face. He got it. He really got it.

-JEROME: I didn't know Wilson's financial condition.

-WILSON: Wilson financial condition doesn't matter.

5. I Tried To Give Away God's Money. Not!

a. My meeting with and connecting to Wilson Chiko in Nairobi, Kenya was a miracle, in and of itself. Prior to departing Germany and headed to Kenya, I basically had two pieces of information. I had where Wilson worked and what days Wilson worked. I knew before I got on the plane to head to Kenyan that the odds were not in our favor to meet or greet each other in Nairobi. Nevertheless, Wilson and I decided to count on a power greater than us to make this connection come to pass. With the help of strangers and angels, God opened a door. The folks at Camp Womba stated that they would drive me to Nairobi on one of the mornings they picking up food and pick me up later around noon so I could visit with my friend. This was an answer to prayer. These folks were our angels from God.

b. When I arrived at the University to meet with Wilson, I explained to the gate-keeper who I was and why I was there to see my friend. I was placed in an office and I waited. Not long after waiting, Rose, Wilson's wife walked in. At that moment, I could begin to breathe a little easier. I had brought a large amount of money (over $1,000) for Wilson's ministry. Rose then decided to use the time that we ~~she and I~~ had to wait for Wilson, to bring me up to speed on all the things happening to them since we were last together over ten years ago. And boy did she have a lot to say. She told me about how they didn't have enough money to send the kids to school. She told me how they at times didn't have enough money to pay bills or even eat. She explained how Wilson was only working for a few days of work a week at the university and that money was very short as well.

c. I told Rose that I brought some money for Wilson's ministry and if I don't get to meet him, I will give her the money for him. I also told her that I wanted them to use this money for them and that I would send them more money later, for his ministry.

d. When Wilson walked into room, I hugged him and I cried. This same man who changed my spiritual life in Texas, was now suffering and there was nothing I could do to change this. Wilson and I caught up and shared what we had done since our absence from each other. Wilson told me nothing about his present financial plight. If it weren't for Rose, I would not have known of his fate at all. This silence on his part didn't surprise me. This is just the kind of man Wilson is. He also didn't know what Rose had shared with me when he and I was talking.

e. When I gave Wilson the money I brought, I told him the following. Rose has already explained and shared some what is going on at this time with you and your family. Take this money that I have here and use it for you and your family. When I return to Europe, I will send you some additional money for your ministry. And I did just that.

f. Guess what I learned, later? Wilson still used every penny I gave to him in Kenya for his ministry. I was not a surprised. And getting mad with Wilson ~~from~~ for putting God first over himself and family, wouldn't have done any good either. Wilson is just that kind of man of God. I thought it was okay to redirect the purpose and use of that money which was set aside for ministry and Wilson decided that this was not what God had laid on his heart and Wilson put himself second. Here was God teaching me another valuable spiritual lesson. God doesn't need our money. He needs our obedience.

-JEROME & WILSON: God is going to be faithful, no matter what.

6. From The Motherland To Another Land

a. I gave Wilson the money for his ministry on a Wednesday at the university, by that Friday evening, Wilson and his family were all at the Nairobi Airport, saying good-bye to me. I was the only one in my group that had people at the airport, seeing them off from Nairobi. It was very strange, but it felt so good.

b. Having to see Wilson's kids grown now, just capped off my entire trip. I remember ten year earlier when they were just toddlers/teenagers.

c. I got to share some of the awesome stories which took place on the Safari and the flat tire and the Bible give-a-ways, along with the boys in the local village. I did not want to leave them and I wanted more time to spend with these my friends and adopted family.

d. When I arrived back in Germany after being gone for three weeks, you know that I had a story/stories to tell and I told them to anyone whom would listen.

e. This trip to Kenyan and my experience with the kids of Club Beyond, far exceeded my anticipation and expectations.

f. I had no clue at this time that God had used my tour to Germany and my trip to Nairobi, Kenya to prepare me for my ultimate retirement from the Army at my next duty station.

Chapter Eight

More to learn and more to earn back in the US

-JEROME: Everybody who came with, can't go with you. (Tempestt Smith)

A Change Of Venue:

Due to the military instability in Europe, our mandatory traveling and the deactivating of units, Alice chose to turned down a very nice paying position with the federal government, when we first arrived. This meant, no extra money for three years in Germany. Now that we are back in the States, she can just pick up where she left off, before Germany and financially, we'll be right back on track again. Well, that is not the way things turned out. One of the first things Alice conveyed to me upon our reassignment to Fort Drum, New York from Germany was that she didn't want to work outside of the home anymore. She wanted to stay at-home. Since this was a promise that I had made to her years ago when we got married and I honored her wishes, with no questions asked. Did I want to know why this sudden change of direction? You bet. But I honored my word and I never asked her even till this day why she wanted to stop working outside the home, at that time.

I also realized that this decision on Alice's part was going to greatly affective me as the head-of-household and the primary bread-winning. How was I to make up for this loss of revenue? How was I going to replace it and still keep harmony all around thing? I didn't have the answer, but I knew that I serviced a God that did. So, I started praying. I also worked very hard and tried not to make Alice feel guilty about her decision to not want to work. What good was it to tell her that it was okay and then in turn, through it up in her face?

My initial direction surrounding all of this was to look into a home-based business for at lease, myself. I figured that this would be a win-win for both Alice and the household. It turned out that this was something both Alice and I were interested in and gravitated too. Alice started looking into an in-home daycare service and I started looking at a mortgage reduction business.

While the home-based business idea was going on behind the scene, my everyday military job was showing some signs of unfortunate instability. I quickly recognized that my organization had a leadership problem. The leaders, weren't leading. The folks in charge were afraid of the folks in charge. So, who's running the show? Good question. By the time I found out what and who the problem was, it was already too late, for me. I had become the target and the next scapegoat. That's right. I became the victim. This put me in a very awkward predicament. It got so bad that I was told to either put in my retirement paper or face being relieved of duty. It was now decision time. I knew how to win and what it was going to take to win. Unfortunately, in order for me to win, I had to destroy someone who had been manipulated and abused by the powers that be. My heart couldn't let me do that. My God wouldn't let me do that. Ultimately, If I had won the battle, I would have lost the war. After I prayed, I chose to walk away. This decision, changed everything. And in less than six-month from this incident, I was retired from the United States Army. To my amazement, I hadn't planned to be a civilian for another two-years. I guess God had a different plan. What you think?

JEROME: Remember working with those kids in Germany; lookout?

While doing my research and preparing to transition out of the Army, everything appeared to point to Atlanta, Georgia. Alice and I came up with a game plan, to drop her off in Baltimore; I would then head to Atlanta; and once I landed that corporate job and a place to live, I will then return to Baltimore and come and get her. It all looked good on paper. I had all of the pieces in place. And I even thought God had signed off on it as well. I later discovered that there was more to this than I even had a clue about.

As I was in the process of transitioning out of the Army, I was informing and explaining to one of my fellow soldiers about this exit process and what she should be on the lookout for so that she can maximize her benefits uponher own departure. I then inquired of her about her husband's status, who had retired about three-months earlier. She went on to tell me that he had taken up a position at military-style boot camp for youth in upstate New York. She told me that he loves what he is doing and they are looking for retirees and military affiliated personnel for staffing. I initially thought that this was a nice jester, but I've got a few things in place for Atlanta and that is where I need to stay focused. Then this soldier ~~then~~ reminded me of my time in Germany with Club Beyond and the kids and how I was so success with them. She then suggested that what would it hurt to just go there and at least interview. You might even like it. Guess what? I liked it and they liked me. Sorry Atlanta. They informed me that I would start off as a trail period or per diem to see if things fit or workout for the future. If they did fit, I would probably come on board in about six-month as a full-time paid employee, with benefits. Until that time, I was basically on-call and at their mercy.

Helping Kids Is One Thing, But I Got Some Bills To Pay, Right?

After the dust had settled of me accepting this new position and me inventorying where Alice and I stood, I noticed that I was in a dilemma. I had retired from the Army two-years sooner than I had planned and this new job isn't going to kick in with any real money for at least six-months, if they accept me. Alice isn't working outside the home or inside the home and my home-based business ~~vendor~~ venture was a bust. Oh, and by the way, my bills are piling up and my retirement salary isn't enough.

Everything on the surface; everything with my own eyes was telling me that I must be losing my mind for not going on to Atlanta. Yet, my heart kept telling me that if I walk away from this opportunity now, I may never get a chance like this ever again. It got real financially hard for us those first few years after retirement. We accumulated over $30,000 in credit card charges for basic bills and groceries.

I had no clue as to how or where I was going to get the money we needed to make it from day to day. I didn't know if after six months at this facility whether they going to accept me as full-time employee or not. But what I did know was that the calling that moved me from going to Atlanta, had sent me here and this is where I was supposed to be. This walking by faith is a scary thing, but it forces you to trust God. I had no one and nowhere else to turn too.

Chapter Nine

God Has Got You. Hello!

Chapter 9?: Should I Give My Best Or Will God Settle For Less?

Listen Jerome, it's not God that you are cheating. Think about it?

a. If I am going to be honest, I am not ashamed to say that I truly questioned whether I should have gone to Atlanta or stayed in New York. New York was definitely looking kind of shaky. I also knew that this feeling was based on what I was feeling and not based on what I knew. See, God never fails.

b. In the meantime, God would bless Alice with a financial windfall, which resulted from her family's sale of a piece of property in Maryland. She was mailed her potion of the inheritance to her in New York.

c. During the period of this transaction, we weren't member of or attending a particular church at the time. Nonetheless, we still wanted to disperse the principle 10% of the proceeds to at least a worthy or needy cause. We knew that any local church wouldn't mind us dropping off this money nor would any of the mainstream non-profit ministries would have a problem with our gift giving either. It turned out that the 10% of the total amount came to about $7,000.00. This was nothing to sneeze at, but what would be the right thing to do? Our stewardship was on the line and I wanted to honor God as He had honored us with such a wonderful gift.

d. I initially thought about Wilson and his ministry, but I hadn't spoken to him in a few years. I knew that I did have a phone number that I might be able to reach him. I just wasn't sure of his physical or financial status at the time, but God did.

So, when ~~we~~ Alice and I came in touch with this money, Wilson had personally relocated to the UK to obtain and additional Master's degree, while his family was still living back in Nairobi Kenya, again.

e. When I initially got in touch with Wilson in the UK, I didn't tell him about the inheritance or the 10% proceeds which were available. Nonetheless, I did ask him was there anything that we could do for him while he was furthering his education in the UK. Wilson explained that he really missed his family in Kenya. He also complained about the fact that it was taking him longer to get things done in school because of the following. He was forced to wait in the library for an open computer to create papers and he also had ~~to~~ long waiting times to get on the internet for research. This process was slowing down his term papers due. He also knew that this was only going to get worse when it came time for his dissertation. The more time that he had to wait to use the equipment, in-turn caused him to remain in the UK longer away from his family.

f. Understanding his predicament, the need for a laptop computer could truly put a dent in Wilson's situation. I then thought to myself, that Alice and I could be of some help in this situation. I then asked Wilson about us sending him a computer to help out. Note, I didn't say a new computer, just a computer. Wilson was very elated about this possibility. I was also elated as well. I had a plan to fix this problem. I immediately saw a way of getting to Wilson my old laptop and me getting a new laptop.

g. So, after I had this conversation with Wilson, I then had this brilliant ideal. I will send Wilson my used portable computer and printer, which is a Mac, to help him out. I would then go and buy myself a brand-new computer and printer, which is a Mac. At the time of this revelation, I felt like a genius. It didn't take long for God's Holy Spirit to step in and open my eyes to see that I had an arteria motive to my intentions. Now, when I came up with this initial concept, it sounded great to me. I thought the ideal was fantastic. Forget about the 10% for God. I in turn, was getting me a brand-new computer. Wilson would have a laptop and this will speed up his time and allow him to get home to his family in Kenya, sooner. Not so fast, Jerome.

h. As I prayed about this awesome ideal, I felt God Holy Spirit telling me to slow it down just a bit and think about the big picture. In the world today, in Europe, who has the biggest market share on uses of and in sale of computers period, Mac or Windows? The answer was Windows. I immediately knew then what I had to do.

i. I then went and purchased a brand-new top of the line Toshiba Windows computer, with a wireless portable printer, a Microsoft Office software package, exterior hard-drive, a ream of paper and some additional cables. I pack all of these items in one box and mailed it to Wilson, directly in the UK. Everything came to about $5,000.00

j. When this package arrived in the UK to Wilson, it took him a couple of days before he could call me to say thank you. I made it perfectly clear to him that we didn't send anything extra or special. We sent him the Lord's money, because the tithe belongs to God and God laid it on our heart to bless him with this gift. He just couldn't believe that this special package had come just for him.

k. Then Wilson shared something with me that was unbelievable. Since I sent the package to him directly in the UK, instead of Nairobi, it made all the difference in the world for Wilson on numerous levels. If I had sent this package to Nairobi instead of the UK, one of two things probably would have happened. When the package arrives, it will usually be opened and inspected. Then Wilson would receive a call to come and pick up the package, but not until he would have been required to pay a tribute of tax on that item/s enclosed. In the other scenario, the item or package would have mysteriously turn up lost, never to be found. Wilson was in tears about the fact that he could now take all of these items back to Nairobi in his luggage and not have to worry about any taxes, tribute or it getting lost. I had no clue. I didn' t know, but God knew. This was all a part of God' s plan from the very beginning.

1. In the meantime, Alice did purchase me a brand-new Apple portable computer. I was very appreciative, since the one I possessed was still operational at the time.

-JEROME: God will always have your back if you are a man of integrity

Baby, I Got Your Back

Back to working with the kids. Alice and my first six-months at this correctional facility were very tough on us financially. Even after they hired me on as full-time employee, the money was still a little tight, because of the debt we had previously accumulated, since I retired. Although the inheritance which Alice received helped, we wanted to be wise about our spending and moving forward. We also wanted to treat the inheritance like an extra bonus that we weren't expecting. So, we didn't include it in our daily budget or living expenses. We also tried to come up with creative ways to generate additional income, but always seem to fall short. Since we had two cars, Alice suggested that she should go out and look for a job to help out; even a part-time job. I wasn't feeling that. This step isn't really what she wanted to do and it contradicted what I promised her when we got married that I would do. I thanked her for her earnest effort, but I told her that I wouldn't feel right if she did that. I told her that if I get a part-time job and we are still stuck and she wants to get a job, then that will be okay. Within the next two-weeks, I went out and got two, part-time jobs.

I got one job working as a substitute teacher/detention monitor at a K-12 School and the other job was working with the disabled adults and their families. Both of these jobs were sporadic and they only called you in when they needed you. This gave you the option to sometimes turn them down went necessary. My wife was surprised; but God wasn' t. Both jobs later produced nice blessings for my students/clients and us.

-JEROME: God always reward the faithful. Be faithful.

People Keep Giving You Money

In addition to this wind-fall of two part-time jobs, another door of opportunity opened up for me on and off the job with the kids, as well. As a new full-time employee, the time had come for my first shift-bid. One of the shift that had opened was called the "weekend warrior shift." This meant 16 hours on Saturday, 16 hours on Sunday and 8 hours on Monday. This three-day shift covered your entire 40-hour work week.

I, in addition, was extremely attracted to this 3-day work week. It just so happens that my military disability afforded me the opportunity to go to college full-time, for free and even pays me a personal steepen each month of school, just to attend school in the amount of ($536). This was additional free money. Well, I got the week-warrior shift and I started going to college full-time as well. Needless to say, our financial picture changed big-time and Alice and ~~Alice~~I, had no complaints. I was receiving my military retirement check, my full-time work check, my 2 part-time checks, my college per-diem check and Alice started receiving her social security check and I wasn't tired or burnt-out. Hello!

You would think that this was more than enough financially to be satisfied with and I was. But God didn't stop there. Here I was working a full-time job, two part-time jobs, going to school full-time, and in spite of this entire workload, I also graduated with honors/Cum-Laude, acquiring a BS Degree with a 3.67 GPA. I considered this GPA an amazing achievement all by itself. But God still wasn't finished. I was also inducted into two National Honor Societies. When I decided that I would continue my college education and pursue my Master's Degree, there was something else that I was totally ignorant too at the time. As I sat in the orientation office to set-up my Grad program, the woman across the desk from me, informed me that because I was a minority in the State of New York and graduated with honors from the under-graduate program, I qualified for a $6,000 dollar a semester Fellowship in the Grad Program. I said, "Excuse me?" That correct sir. $6,000 dollar a semester. There is more. In addition to this extra money, I also qualified for student loan money. So, I took the student loan money that I was still eligible for and paid off all my credit card debt of over $35,000 dollars. All of the interest on the student loan is tax deductible. The interest on the credit card debt, was not. I'm still paying off the student loan as I'm writing this book and I'm still getting the tax-deductible benefit, today.

With all that I have already shared with you, God still wasn't finished blessing me. As I transitioned from undergraduate to graduate, I notified the K-12 school that I would no longer be substituting or doing detention. I wanted to focus specifically on my graduate work and my grades. The principal at the school understood and I went on about my business. Then out of nowhere, I receive a call from the new principal of that same school. It appears that the old principal told her about how I revolutionized the detention program on my own and had very few kids coming to detention at all. She called me into her office to offered me my old job back. I said thanks, but no thanks. I made it clear that all I wanted to do was focus on my studies in Grad school, without any distractions. She then made me an offer that I could not refuse. She asked me to come back and take over the detention program, but for us to turn it into and internship for college and we will pay you as well. I then approached my department head about a paid verses non-paid internships. His attitude was that as long as you do the work, I don't care if you get paid or not. That's right, you guess it, I was back at that school two days a week as their detention monitor. Here is what really blew me away about this particular set-up. I was helping the school. I was helping the students. I was getting paid money from the school. I was getting college credit. And I was using the detention period to study for my college classes. Talk about double-dipping. I was left speechless. When I shared this chain of events with my wife Alice, she responded, "Somebody is always giving you money." I responded, "Is that a problem?" She just shook her head and walked away.

Jerome: I tried to put God last on purpose

One more miraculous thing took place as a result of that weekend-warrior shift. At the facility with the kids, Saturday and Sunday were like their down time. So, on Sunday's they had at least one-hour of religious time. The Sunday religious time on the schedule was headed up by a local Chaplain from the community. For whatever reason, he left. This left an opening in Sunday schedule. The kids approached me about take over this part of the Sunday schedule. I told the kids reluctantly, that I am honored and would love to do their religious time. That's right, I said reluctantly. Nevertheless, I made it clear to the kids that I would not approach the leadership and ask to take over for fear they might think I am trying to get out of work. The kids then approached the leadership of the facility, and they gave their blessing. Then on Sunday's I was conducting the religious time. Although I am a Christian, I made it very clear that this was their religious time, and not mine. We will respect each other in here and we will respect each other's differences. As the facilitator, I made it clear to them that I as a Christian, I have only one authority. That authority is the Word of God. When you asked me a question, I will not give you my opinion. I will give you God's Word. I told them that every Sunday that I arrive that I will come prepared with a lesson plan to teach them. But let me make something very clear. "The lesson plan is always option. But the Word of God is never option." I encouraged them to speak to each other and exchange ideas. Yet, it seemed to me that the question was always being directed to me. I would in turn, give them God's Word. I did this for about two-years and as much as I tried to purposely suppress and keep God second. Nevertheless, He came out first, anyway. He always comes out first. I purposely conducted things this way so that no one could accuse me of trying to openly proselytize these kids. Another of the things that truly amazing me about these gathering where the fact that I could only hold 20-students per class. When the time came for the Religious Time on Sundays, initially, I only had about 5-6 kids. As time passed and the group grew, I was forced at times to turn kids away, because I didn't have enough room in the class to accommodate them all. What a problem to have.

As I stopped to really take inventory, I knew that I was a blessed man. I was reaching these at-risk kids face-to-face. In addition, the government was not only giving me a free education, they were paying me to get the education as well. And if that weren't enough, I was even reaching these kids on a spiritual level. I could not have asked for more. Nevertheless, God didn't stop there. In the background of all of this positive activity, God was still working. After these kids six-months at this facility, these kids had another six-months of after-care in New York City. This after-care was the test to see if anything at the facility took so that they could/would make it back in New York City. 3-6 months after departing my facility, I started receiving phone calls from the After-care program, from these same kids. Too many of them had me in tears telling how my impact basically saved their lives. I was left speechless. I had no reasonable explanation for these phone calls. Notwithstanding, I was eternally grateful. This was that one-on-one confirmation that I was truly making a difference. I was definitely changing lives. Thank you, God

-JEROME: I had gotten too close.

When You Refuse To Move, God Will Make You Move.

Am I going to tell you all of the wonderful things that God has done for me, to me and through me as result of working with these at-risk kids? No. But I will say this, I kept getting phone call, after phone call, telling me how I literally saved their lives. You can only imagine how I felt and what that meant me to under those circumstances. I even got visit from family-member who asked to speak with me personally during facility visits. Their stories were amazing. If you would like to hear more details about my seven-year journey with these kids, checkout my book, **"Fixing The Broken, Without Being Broken Book 1"** and I will give you all of the sorted details. It's a three-part series. Notwithstanding, as my relationship with those kids increased, my relationship with leadership and fellow staff, decreased. Things got very political and polarizing. I became a big problem because I wouldn't play the game. They seem to try and throw everything at me as well. It got even more ugly as the days went by. Yet, I wasn't afraid nor was I intimidated by the allegations and tactics that were used to try and silence and suppress me. Some of the staff had to learn the hard way that I am not easily intimated or frightened. I come from the streets and the streets show you how to survive. Things got so ugly that some of the staff started disrespecting me right in front of the kids. I tried to blow it off and pretend that certain things weren't happening. These kids were too smart. They saw right through it. It got to the point that the kids were telling the staff that we will listen to Sergeant Redd, but we won't listen to you. As much as I tried to warn these kids not to do that, here's where they wouldn't listen to me. As they started getting written up and were given more time on their sentence, I cried out to God about the fairness of what was going on. God, confronted me with a question? "Jerome, is this about you or is this about the kids?" I said, you know that it is about the kids. His response was, then you know what you have to do." I immediately submitted my resignation. The Facility Director's mouth fell open.

They tried to do everything in their power to get rid of me; they even tried to railroad me out of this place and couldn't and now I'm leaving voluntarily? What is going on? I'll tell you what is going on. God is going on.

I wanted to save all the kids. I wanted them all to be treated fairly. I wanted to walk away on my terms. All of these attributes are honorably and commendable. And the day I voluntarily walked away from this facility, I was in tears and I felt like and utter failure. In reality, I wasn't. But I wasn't strong enough or big enough, at that time, to see the big picture. It wasn't until years later that God opened my eyes to see that my 3-book series on this chain-of-events is going to touch a whole lot of people. I guess, I wasn't such a failure after all?

Chapter Ten

Out Of My Comfort Zone

-JEROME: Remember, the kids to told you first, how good you were.

What next God?

After resigning from New York, I dropped everything and moved back to my hometown of Baltimore. I had no job lined up or financial system in place before I departed New York. God said leave and in less than thirty days, I was gone. In addition, I also knew that my retirement check and Alice retirement check, wasn't going to pay all of the bills. With the help of a good friend and Christian, I started working at an engineering firm, teaching during the week and selling hand-blown glass on the weekend. The selling of this hand-blown glass is how I met the publisher of my 3-poetry books. That's right poetry. I've been writing poetry since I was a teenager. While working with those kids in New York, I shared some of my poetry with them. I was asked by the kids at the time, was I published? I said no. I responded that I just do this on the side for fun. I was told by more than one of those kids that my poetry was good enough to be published. A few years later, my publisher was saying the same thing. The first book did very well. In less than 2-years, I sold over 3,000s copies. Then one book, turned into 3-books.

-JEROME: Where is your safety net? God is my safety net.

From Author To Entrepreneur

The positive part-time sale of these books, eventually opened up another door. I figured out that if I worked as hard on a full-time basis selling these books as I was working on a part-time basis selling them, I should be able to match, if not exceed my present full-time working salary at the engineering firm. Since I have always been one to preach that you should always work for and pay one's self, instead of others, I was compelled to approach the owner of the firm, with an ultimatum. Not two weeks, but I would give him six months to find a replacement for me and then I would leave and step out on my own. He thanked me for the heads-up. When I shared this information with my wife Alice, she didn't demonstrate the same appreciation as the owner. In fact, her response kind of caught me off guard. She said, "You've got a full-time job, with full-time benefits and a 5% match on your 401K; you going to work." Wow!

After all the dust had settled over her statement, I share with her the following. I reminded her of my time with those boys in New York. I told her how I told them that it was okay to go to school and get a good job and do well on that job. But I also told them that they should always work themselves out of that job. Why? Because no one is ever going to pay you what your worth, but you. I then shared with my wife how that this chance was affording me the opportunity to live what I preached. I told her that if I don't do this, I would be a hypocrite. If I don't do this, I'm fake. If I don't do this, I'll die. And if I can't live with myself, I damn sure can't live with you. I'm not asking for your permission. I am keeping you informed. That last statement was the mic-drop. My mind and decision had already been made up and having a discussion about it wasn't going to change my direction or decision. She and I could discuss this as much as she desired, but my mind was made up and we both knew it.

Five-months into this six-month decision, the owner of the firm approached me and asked me was I still planning on leaving? I replied that I had no choice in the matter. I had already put my foot in my mouth. I would be leaving for good in one-month. To my amazement and shock, the owner made the following offer. Why don't you become a part-time employee or a Contractor? This way you only have to come in and teach when we need you and the rest of the time, you can sell your books. Prior to his suggestion, I hadn't even considered this as an option. This made it a win-win-win situation for everybody and I said yes. Even my wife could really appreciate this gift about six-months later as she was doing the household bills and seeing the nice increase on all levels due to more income. The real sweet thing about all of this was, I was working less hours and making more money. This afforded me the opportunity to investigate other means of acquiring additional income as well. I then decided to increased my involvement and pursuit in the direct-sale and multi-level-marketing businesses.

Chapter Eleven

Will The Real Jerome Redd, Please Stand-up?

-JEROME: A different look at the employment realm and expanding my creativity.

Taking inventory after I retired from the Army up to now.

a. I was very successful at that youth facility, working with the at-risk kids. You might say that I was a little too successful. I quickly discovered that I was really good at reaching these kids and making a difference. In fact, I was too good. I was so good that I became compelled to put in my resignation and leave. My next stop would be Baltimore, Maryland.

b. Due to that success with the kids in New York, I thought that when I arrived back home that I would end up doing something with or surrounding kids, like I did in New York. Instead, I go to work for an engineering firm, teaching classes to licensed professional.

c. In addition, I also ended up writing 3 books of poetry; restarted my acting career; started my stand-up comedy career; working in my spare time to acquire residual income and stepped down from my full-time employment to become a contractor with the same firm. I also during this 15-year-period, started working on a book about those kids in New York, but could never seem to get it completed. Nevertheless, I still stayed in touch with my friend Wilson and contributed to his ministry, from time-to-time.

d. As my spiritual life continued to grow, I felt this urge and desire to go back to Nairobi and visit my friend Wilson again, just because. There was no particular reason. It appeared that in those last five years, that my desire to go and visit Wilson, grew stronger and stronger. This posed a question? Why was my desire to go visit him growing stronger and stronger over time? I did not have a specific reason or answer for this pressing question, until recently.

e. As I have been continuing my efforts to pursue residual income, God had to use someone close in my life to show me that I was slightly off course in reference to the direction that God wanted me to go in. I was looking outside of myself, when in fact, I should have been looking within.

f. God brought a young lady into my life to reveal to me something that I was not aware of nor even had a clue this even existed. God used this woman to first reveal that I was not just an average person. And that I wasn't an average Christian either. And the gifts that God had given to me were greatly underused and under acknowledged, on my part. God use her to show me that I brought a skill-set to the table that most people can't even touch. This young lady looked me in the eyes and said, "You don't get it, Jerome." And she was right. Not only didn't I get it, Secondly, I wasn't giving myself enough credit for the skills and gifts that God had bestowed upon me. It appeared that I was compartmentalizing my assets one at a time or may two, while she and others saw the whole package. They saw multiple skills and abilities. Once God got her to open my eyes so that I could see the same things that she did, nothing in my life has been the same since then; nothing.

g. As I have ~~just~~ turned sixty-years-old, my life has started picking up instead of slowing down. But it is now picking up for a specific reason and purpose. And I like what I see and hear coming from this increase. Don't get me wrong, not everybody agrees with my new vision. Here's the deal, I'm not soliciting everybody's opinion. I don't need everybody's opinion. I only need one person's opinion. His name is God.

h. At the end of 2016, I heard the Holy Spirit speak to my soul the following: "Your artistry and your creativity, will determine your prosperity." When I decide to act on this notion and receive this notion, some strange things started to happen.

-JEROME: You can't take God at His Word and expect things to just remain the same.

Chapter Twelve

Guess What? That Which You Were Seeking Was There All The Time

-JEROME: What do you mean, "I need to go to Kenya?"

It's time to go to Ninivah.

a. I shifted gears and began to slow down and move away from the direct marketing and multi-level marketing entities that I was spending a lot of time with. I immediately started back on my book about the kids in New York State. I also focused on some other books that I was interested in writing. I started looking more deeply into being a motivational speaker.

I also wanted to pull together some poems for my fourth poetry book.

b. At the start of 2017, I noticed that my plate was running over and there were a lot more responsibilities that had fallen into my lap, along with the usual. But I also noticed that I wasn't dealing with everything the same way I had done before either. For some reason, I was handling one thing after another and handling it well. Now of course, I would like to take credit for this progress, but if I did, that would be a down-right lie, on my part. I knew in my heart of hearts, Who was really behind all of these things, changes and even the improvements in my life. It was God and God alone.

c. With all the changes that were going on in my personal, spiritual and professional life, I had one more thing to add to the plate. In January 2017, my mother had a fire in her home and she came to live with my wife and I. If you didn't know, I'm a mamma's boy and my wife knew this when she married me. My mother stayed one year and two months before she returned home. My wife took care of my mom as if she were her own mom. My wife's care for my mother was impeccable. I am truly a blessed man.

d. In addition, the following also happened. I went back to review my manuscript that I had written a few years ago about the kids in New York and was trying to decide on which direction to move in as it pertained to this draft. It just so happens that I had purchased a program on-line that shows you how to write a book from scratch. Seeing I already had an 84-page manuscript done and partially completed, this was going to be a cake walk, right? Wrong. So, I decided to put the manuscript aside and follow the initial instructions as if I didn't have a manuscript at all. I discovered very quickly one of the reasons why I was having trouble getting this book done. I concluded that this book needed to be written into at least two books and not one. I was flabbergasted. I later changed that to a 3-book series.

e. Revelations like what happened with taking the manuscript from a 1-book to a 3-books series, came straight from the pages of when Wilson Chiko and I were just walking by faith, from day to day. Watching and witnessing how God compelled Wilson to step out on faith, had influenced me to follow in Wilson's, very footsteps. I wasn't afraid of the future and I wasn't afraid of the consequences. I knew Who was in charge and Who had my back at all times.

f. I also noticed something else that was taking place in my commentary as I moved from place to place and meeting up with different people along life's journey. I realized that not only was I talking more about Wilson, people wanted to know more about where my boldness and faith walk was coming from. I had to give credit where credit was due. This walk became solidified during those times and periods that I was hanging out and around Wilson Chiko, in Texas.

g. Then one day I was sitting in my Accountant's office. She is a Christian. I was sharing with her this story about how I felt that God was urging me to go and visit my friend in Kenya again. But I also told her that I'm not sure why my feeling keeps getting stronger and stronger. I then told her one of the stories that I have spoken and shared with others countless times about Wilson going to Abilene, instead of going to Houston. You could see that she was visibly moved by the story and so was I. I also realized at that very moment that all of the other people whom I had told this story to in the past were also visibly moved. It was at that very moment that I heard the Holy Spirit speak to me about my future destiny with Wilson and Kenya. The Spirit made it clear that I was going to write a book about Wilson Chiko and how he changed my Christian life. He also made it clear that the ending of this book was not going to be written until after I traveled to Kenya and returned. I thought I was going crazy or losing my mind. It is possible that I could be mistaken and I'm just saying this as an excuse for whatever reason? Not!

h. I then began to have a dialogue with God's Holy Spirit. I said, "Are You listening to my accountant? Between the State of Maryland and the IRS, I owe nearly $20,000 dollar in back income taxes that I don't have. Where am I going to get the money to fly to Kenya and of course, I can't go there, empty handed and broke. I've got to bring something for his ministry.

i. Without going into details, Thirty-days later, I was boarding a plane to Nairobi Kenya with a brand-new laptop, brand-new tablet, MS software and $3080, in cash to take to Wilson Chiko. And I still owed the government $20,000 dollars in back tax money, at the time. Since God didn't explain to me how He did this, I have no way of explaining to you how He did this. All I know is that it happened and it is marvelous in our eyes.

-JEROME: There's a problem, but money isn't it. Who knew?

Chapter Thirteen

It's Seatbelt Time

Nairobi, Kenya. The Rest Of The Story

On March 31, 2017, I departed from Dulles International Airport, bound for Kenya and scheduled to return on April 9, 2017. I knew something special was going to happen, I just didn't have a clue as to what that special thing really was. I journaled every-day I was in Kenya and something special/crazy/miraculous, happened each and every day I was there.

BEFORE THE TRIP:

a. One of God's confirmations to me that He was in the driver's seat on this entire project, came by the way of me writing the outline for this book itself. Since I was only going to receive the ending once I got to Kenya, everything else, I should already have, and I did. So, I sat down and wrote out initially, ~~nineteen~~ all the chapters of the book ahead of time, in outline form. And since I knew for the most part what was going to go into each chapter, I wrote a little extra for each chapter in the outline itself. For this book, the average outline should have been between 4-5 pages for15-19 chapters. I made the outlines 14 pages, 8 ½ X 11. It was more than just an outline. It was basically a pamphlet with bullet points. I was very impressed.

b. I week before I departed on this trip, I emailed Wilson my itinerary and called him to confirm everything. He asked me was I sure I was coming? I told him to check his email for my non-refundable plane tickets. He then told me that since I was coming that he has coordinated with his Pastor to have me teach the Sunday School lesson and in addition, bring the morning message to the church. Remember, he didn' t ask me, he told me. I responded. "I ain' t scared of you. Bring it on. I already know what the morning message is going to be. " We both laughed. Oh by the way, Wilson has never heard or seen me preach.

c. To ensure to me beyond a shadow of a doubt that it was God Who had put this entire trip together, here is what happened on my way to the airport on the day of my departure. When I departed Baltimore, headed to DC, I thought Dulles and Reagan were the same airport. After I parked my car at Reagan and was catching the shuttle bus to the terminal, was when the bus driver tells me that my flight was leaving from Dulles and not Reagan. This was a very interesting revelation.

d. After returning to my car, I then drove to Dulles, in the rain, rush hour traffic and had never been there before. After parking again, I checked-in, hit TSA and immigration's. As I finally arrived at my gate, the plane to Nairobi was boarding. As I sat in my seat, covered in sweat and disbelief of what had just taken place, I asked God this very question. "What just happened?" This alone was a miracle all by itself. How in the world did I make it onto this flight? Wow!

e. They fed me 4-times on this 13-hour flight to Ethiopia. I truly enjoyed it.

f. When I arrived in Ethiopia, everything was initially on scheduled. But the flight to Nairobi was canceled and there was no announcement. When I finally got the right information, the next flight wasn't until 8 hours from then. They wanted to put me on a bus and take me to a hotel and then bring me back. I said no thanks, I'll wait in the terminal and relax.

g. I called Wilson and told him about the delay and don't come to the airport to early. Oh, and my cell phone was not working either. I had to pay to make a call to Wilson. Later that evening, I arrived in Nairobi and Wilson and Rose were waiting for me at the airport. Everything in customs went smooth, except for being in the wrong line and God took care of that as well. So, I was glad to be back safe in the Motherland.

JEROME ON THE GROUND:

a. My time on the ground with Wilson was filled with nothing less than miracle- impactful days for the entire time I was in Kenya. God held nothing back. He completely blind-sided me and show me great and marvelous things.

b. The first event was when I arrived at Wilson's house. I give him the gifts that God gave me for him. I gave him a brand-new laptop, with software; a brand-new tablet for preaching and $3,080 in cash. This is equivalent to over $300,000.00 in Kenyan Shillings. This was a lot of money.

c. After everyone went to bed and it was just Wilson and I sitting at his kitchen table talking about the goodness of God, it hit me. I told Wilson that it was about thirty-years ago that he and I were sitting at his kitchen table in Abilene, Texas and him telling me about the miraculous efforts of God on his behalf when it seemed like every door in Abilene was closed, but all the door in Houston were open. Yet Wilson, you chose Abilene. And I told God that day that I wanted the faith that Wilson had, because I would have gone to Houston instead. I then told Wilson that thirty-days ago, and flat-broke, the Holy Spirit told me to come to Kenya and see a man named Wilson Chiko. Well, I'm here and I didn't come broke. God had molded and made me the servant that He wanted me to be so that I would move in spite of my circumstance. I told Wilson that the Holy Spirit had confirmed to me that I was not ready to go to Abilene back then. But that I now have the kind of faith that Wilson Chiko has. Wilson and I, both cried at the acknowledgment of this revelation. It was as if God was telling me that I am now ready ~~to~~ for the Abilene's of life.

d. On Sunday morning, the next day, before church, I got to ministered to Wilson's daughter and her son. During church, I taught the Sunday School lesson and Wilson interpreted it. During the morning worship, I preached the morning message and the Pastor interpreted it. In both the class and the sermon, I spoke about spreading the Gospel. I also spoke about how Wilson was instrumental in helping me grow in my quest for spreading the Gospel. Then I dropped the bomb on everybody, including Wilson and his family. I then announced publicly that I was writing a book about this journey with Wilson and that once it gets published that a potion of the proceeds from the sale of each book will come to Wilson, for his ministry. It was truly a mic-dropping moment. The Pastor let Wilson and Rose speak, but they were caught totally off-guard as well. That's how God works. Later, Wilson's wife Rose asked him did he know about this? And he said no. I told Wilson that this wasn't my idea. It was God's idea. I told him how God provoked me to come and to also write the book.

e. During this week, I got to visit Day Star University twice. This is where Wilson works as a professor. The second time I visited the university, Wilson let me speak to two of his classes at the end of the class. Wilson, the students and I were blown away, by the reaction of the students to my presence in the classroom. When the second session was over, I asked Wilson, "What just happened?" His response was "I don't know." I then responded that neither did I. His students were all over me, with questions and inquiries and disbelief that they were actually talking to me. I was so humbled and grateful at the same time.

f. While still in recovery mode from what happened at the college, God had something else He needed for me to know. Every morning when I wake up in Kenya around 5am, I would journal about what had happened to me previously. Upon my arrival in country,

I learned from Wilson that there had been a drought there for two-years. So, after the incident in school with the students, I went to bed like I normally do. The next morning, God wakes me up by the falling of rain on the roof top. I initially thought I was dreaming and went back to sleep. God then increase the rain and the volume, which compels me to get out of bed. I now knew that this is not a dream and that this was not an accident. I arose from my sleep and I was about to start journaling like I normally do, the Holy Spirit said stop and pay attention. God began to minister to me and share with me a vision. He let me see that my vision wasn't as big as His vision. He also made it clear that I wasn't going to just help Wilson, but that we would ultimately become business partner in the Gospel. When the Spirit of God finished speaking to me, He said that it was okay now for me to write it down and I then started journaling. I then went to Wilson before he went work and told him what happened. Wilson, like myself, had nothing to say. We were both speechless.

g. I also got to spend some time with Wilson's grandson, Baracka. He is what I would call, a mini-genius. I was blown away every time I got a chance to exchange in conversation with him. As I was about to depart Kenya, I told Wilson and I told ~~his~~ Baracka's mother that he stole my heart and that I will be back to get it or him. What an amazing young man.

h. The last night I spend at Wilson's house, he had each one of us go around the room and explain or narrate what my visit meant to them. I ~~got~~ was able to get through everyone except Baracka, okay. He crushed me and had me in tears. He gave me far more credit than I deserved, and I am so thankful.

i. The next day, I was back on a flight headed home to the US.

AFTER THE TRIP:

a. With all that had taken place on those seven days, you better believe that the I was on cloud-nine and that everybody was going to know about it. And I tried to tell everybody. Wilson also sent thank you letters to those who gave money and contributed.

b. I first reached out on social media. I release about four posts on Facebook over the next month.

c. Of course, I beat up friends, family and fellow Christians about this wonderful experience.

d. I also approached my Pastor at the time, Marshall F. Prentice of Zion Baptist Church Baltimore, Maryland. When he heard this story, he said, "Jerome, you need to speak to the congregation," and I did. I made it clear that you don't have go all the way to Kenya to hear God's voice, but He didn't call you to just sit in those pews either. What an amazing man of God to let me speak to his flock. But that is just the kind of man he is. The Gospel must come first.

e. The overall feedback from individuals, Christians, Pastors, Facebook was all positive. With that said, I was ready to kick this into high-gear. Not!

Chapter Fourteen

3-Years Has Passed Since Kenya, Is God Sleep?

Jerome: Sometimes your timing, isn't God's timing.

I quickly ran into a slight dilemma. I told Wilson that as soon as I finished my kid's book and got it published, that I would have the financial resource to get his book published. I wasn't worry about this because the trip to Kenya had me motivated and writing about those kids in New York was on my heart.

After about eight months of writing the kids book, I was supposed to be finished. I wasn't. I knew something was missing. I knew something was wrong.

Nevertheless, I had no clue what it was that was wrong. So, I took the kid's book and I sat it to the side. I knew that I was not going to put out any junk. I also knew that I wasn't going to put it out until I knew it was ready. Yet, in the meantime, Wilson's book was still on hold and still not written. At this time, I went into deep prayer mode. If God is not the author of confusion, why am I stuck in this position? If I am going to be honest, God did answer this question when I thought He should have answered it. But, He did answer it? I felt like the kid's book had too much in it at the time and that what I wanted to say, might get lost in translation in its present form. I believe that God agreed, and it went from one book, into two books. And it is now a 3-book series. This means that all three books get the same treatment as ~~on~~ the one book. This also means that this is three times the revenue to publish all three at the same time as well. I then went back to rewriting the kid's books. So, God was not asleep. I was just a little slow.

I am now extremely excited about the possibilities and the direction that my kid's books are taking and I got ~~to~~ work to do. I am making and made very good progression with it. Book one of the kid's book, finally went to the editor. The editor completed the mission. The book looked fantastic. But, there is only one problem though. I ran out of money to finish paying off the editor for this first book. In addition, I don't have the revenue to have the other two books, edited either. Editing is usually the most expensive part/potion of the publishing process.

Well, we know that God was not sleep and the editor definitely, takes cash. With all that said, everything slows down again. So, now I'm looking for the money to pay off the editor, for book one and trying organize both books 2 and 3, so when the funds are available, I can get them edited as well. In the meantime, it is coming up on the Christmas holiday and I get and invitation from my Nephew in Iowa to come and visit. I am extremely tempted to go because at his home on the Eastern Shore last year, I was able to finish book 2 of the kid's book at his place. So, I asked myself, can lighting strike twice? Will this be the same type of environment for when I completed book 2 for the kids? I had to take a chance and I brought a ticket for my wife and I. And let me tell you, I was not disappointed.

Chapter Fifteen

I Didn't See It Coming

Jerome: I wasn't ready

A damaged computer spawned the writing of a book and poetry.

Before departed Baltimore to head to Iowa, Jerome ordered a used MacBook Pro from off-line. He picked up the used computer around two-days before departing for Iowa. Jerome figured that he would disconnect his portable external hard-drive and take it to Iowa with him and have access to all of his creative file at his finger-tips. As Jerome opened the shipment, plugged in and pushed the start button on the computer, he got nothing. After about an hour of playing around and switching power cords, it was obvious that the power source to this computer wasn't working. And although he was able to return the item, before departing for Iowa, he still had a problem. He still didn't have a personal laptop to take to Iowa. His backup plan was to take his company computer and use it. But the problem with this situation was that the company computer wasn't compatible with Jerome's external hard-drive. Besides, it would need to be formatted if it was to be used and that hasn't been authorized by his employer.

Considering this dilemma, Jerome decided to take the important documents from the external hard-drive and put them on a portable jump drive. Jerome, later discovered because this was being done at the last minute, that some of the files didn't get transferred. This in turned posed a slight problem. Some flies were completely left behind, while others were only partially left behind. Two of the projects that he was hoping to address on this trip, weren't accessible or not on the jump-drive at all. None of that mattered. Jerome could at least get books 2&3 of his kid's books ready for the editor, while on vacation. Right?

Despite these computer setbacks, Jerome's creativity started on his first flight out of BWI airport, headed to Iowa. That's when he completed his first poem. By the time ~~he~~ Jerome arrived in Iowa, he had written 5 new poems. When Jerome got to his Nephew's house, it was about 2pm. He then inventoried the entire house from top to bottom so he could stake out a location to create in. He found that spot in the dining room on the first floor. After setting up his spot, Jerome inventoried his jump-drive to discover his hidden problems. Jerome then decided that if he didn't bring what he had planned to bring, he was going to find something to work on that would prove to be profitable while here. Instead of working on the 3-book series, Jerome decided to work on Wilson's book. Since he had the outlined it from three years ago and had beefed up all the chapters for each of them outlined, and coupled with his notes after the trip, he now had a starting place.

This decision to work on Wilson's book, produces some unintended results. I had only decided to work on a couple of chapters from Wilson's book. I started this on Tuesday night and by Thursday night, all 3-outlineed chapters were completed. In three days, I had 32 pages 8 & ½ X 11. (With a word-count 18600). When I had finished in 3-days, my only comment was, if God can do this much in 3-days, image what He going to do over the next 3-weeks, while I'm here. When I finished those chapters, the only thing that was basically missing was the beginning and the ending of the book. I couldn't believe what God had just done. I continued to scrub, revises and update what I had already written. At day 5, it is up to 38 pages and 21,506 word-count. By time Jerome got home and included the additional trip information, it is now 47 pages, 26,485 word-count. In addition, I also wrote an individual 20-lined poem for everyday that I was in Iowa. That ~~was~~ turned out to be twenty brand-new poems. This is crazy.

What I also think is so crazy about all of this is that the writing of this book at this time was my back-up plan. And I had only plan to do a few chapters. Nevertheless, it was God's planned purpose for me, all the time. What I quickly discovered was that God did a switch-a-rue on me. I was hoping to work on and have my 3-book series ready for publishing after this vacation. Since I already have one book edited, I now only need the other 2 books, edited. And the other things needed are only a formality. Not only did God have me doing the Wilson's book, He had me to change the initial direction that I had planned to go in with this book, when I wrote the original outline.

In the outline, I wrote each chapter as a short story, with ~~very~~ just a little bit of commentary. The chapters would then provoke and require that you make your own decision about the right and the wrong for each one. These chapters compelled you to question your status as it pertains to salvation and/or the journey. I also realized that God had figured out a way to get me to deliver this manuscript differently than how I had intended too. I was was telling one of my friends that if I knew that God wanted me to write a book about the significance of salvation itself, I probably wouldn' t have written it. There is already a Book out there about Salvation. It' s called the Bible. That' s right, I said it.

Chapter Sixteen

Jerome: Somebody call the authorities, I got tricked.

Wait a minute, I wrote the outline for this book over three years-ago, with the thought that it was going to be about the life of Wilson Chiko and how that impacted me? But fast-forward, this same outline, in fact is a collection of stories about the lives of some obedient Christians, who just wanted to serve their God, right? I believe that since God knew that I had no desire to write book about salvation, He inspired me to write a book about the journey of a man who is saved and is growing from day to day in his own personal walk with God. God also had me stick myself inside these pages as an eye-witness testimony to the truth of the entire matter and to learn a few things in the process.

Now that God has tricked me into writing this book, I am also humbled and honored that He even chose me. I am also amazed that He chose Wilson as well. And then He combined our lives together, so that others might clearly see that this is not a joke or has been made up to impress or shun others. This is the true account of our lives over a forty-year span. Our growth and maturity during this entire span is nothing less than a miracle in and of itself. But guess what? We also took you along for the ride as well. We gave you a snapshot and an overview of the working of God in our lives and just how crazy it can really be. Yet, we never considered quitting as an option. We were sad at times. We were sick at times. We were at our wits end and with no money at times. Nevertheless, He kept His promises over and over and over again. He said, "I will never leave you nor forsake you." In all of my years of walking hand-in-hand with God, I cannot recall one incident, where I was felt left or abandoned. He also has always had a plan for me. It was I, who needed the back-up plan/s. God's plan/s worked every time. There is a scripture which reads, "I once was young, but now I am old. Neither have I seen the righteous forsaken, nor His seed begging bread." In addition, I have never heard Wilson complain either.

What truly amazes me about this entire story goes back to my youth. As a young man growing up in America, I always heard and were told stories about American's whom left the US as missionaries for South America, the Middle East, Africa, Asia and brought the Gospel there and changed lives. Then one day, I met a man named Wilson Chiko, from one of those countries and he in turn, changed my life. I thought that I just had to tell his story and I did. But, I later learned that his story, wasn't about him. His story was about the one Whom called him in the beginning. When I called Wilson on the phone to explain to him how the narrative of this story about him had changed in context, he jumped for joy. I explained to him that this explanation was a commentary about obedience and service to God, Wilson was a very happy man to hear this.

As I reflect back on each step that I took and on each pursuit that I embraced, it involved a lot of faith. It took a lot of courage and it took a lot of setting aside what I was feeling within. I also believe that the same applied to my friend, Wilson. When I examined my accomplishments with faith and without faith, with faith won every time. There were times when I even felt like a fool and couldn't articulate to others what was going on, but I couldn't stop. At times, I thought I was being tricked, but somehow and some way, the light always would shine through and I was grateful. I'm going to share who you guys a little secret. Every time I would step out on faith with preconceived notions, I fell short. This taught me in time, to keep trusting the process. Don't get me wrong. I still have intimate conversations with God about what I should and shouldn't do on my daily journey. But His consistency has proven to me that once our conversation is done, it is time for Jerome to move. Is it painful sometimes, yes? Is it depressing sometimes, yes? Is it confusing at times, yes? But He never failed me; not one time. I don't always know what to do or to take on each journey, but what I never leave behind is my faith. It is like my American Express Card. I don't leave home without it.

Chapter Seventeen

Jerome & Wilson: The Real Journey

In this book, Wilson and I, shared our journey. Wilson and I are both still on our journey. Now, what about your journey? I spoke earlier about taking your own journey, but I also wanted you to first take a look at this snap-shot of us. If you look real close, you will see that this is a blueprint for Wilson and Jerome. It is not a blueprint for you. It is not a blueprint for others. It is only an example of how or the means with which the blueprint got created in the first place. Each individual must create and participate in their own blue-print. They must participate in their own relationship with God, which is a one-on-one deal. Others can and others will come along side, but it must start with a one-on-one commitment to God and God alone. When that takes place like it is supposed to be, it undoubtedly helps to eliminate distractions and confusion. It even helps you to know when you are speaking; when others are speaking; or whether God is speaking. Note: The steps of a righteous man are ordered by the Lord.

You can't walk in our shoes. You have to walk in your own shoes. But we have given you a road map of what that journey can and does look like. With that said, what are you going to do on your trip? Wilson and I can't take your trip for you or tell you how to manage things on your trip. We allowed God to establish a personal relationship with us and then we let Him continue with us as we took this crazy journey of life. We had no clue as to what to expect or what was over the next hill. We just knew that God was a rewarder of those who diligently seek Him. So, guess what we did? We let go and we let God. And then the rest became our his-story. So, what will be your history when it is all said and done? Will you afford someone else a snapshot, an overview or a peek into your spiritual life and a walk with God? Will you leave a legacy that someone else can grab a hold of and know that it is solid, sustainable, and rooted deeply in the Rock of Heaven? Please take an inventory before you disperse your spiritual experience to others. If I'm going to be honest, I don't believe that either Wilson or I believed that we were worthy to carry this load. But guess what? God thought we were worthy and that is good enough for me.

I want you to be able to pass on your spiritual legacy as freely as I have passed on mine in this book. I have nothing to be ashamed of or afraid of. I made mistakes. I miss-read God's directions at times and at other times I was down-right disobedient. Guess what? He never stopped loving and caring for me. He always showed me the way of escape. He always gave me options. He never forced Himself upon me. He never made me do the right thing. In retrospect, I believe that God should get His head examined for all of the chances He gave me time and time again. Then I read about how He cast my sins in the sea of forgetfulness, never to be remembered. I believe that God gave me a life that is worth living and worth sharing. It is not expendable. Please pass this manuscript on to someone else. Yet, my ultimate hope and ultimate pray would be that you be able to live a life that is worthy to pass on and share with others as well. Thank you.

Connect With Me

Contact Information For Jerome Redd

Website: www.letsthinkchangegrow.com

Email: jredd@letsthinkchangegrow.com

Email: glasspoetry@gmail.com

Facebook:

https://www.facebook.com/jeromeromey.redd/

Twitter: https://twitter.com/JeromeRedd

https://www.instagram.com/jomeredd7/

https://www.linkedin.com/in/jerome-redd-a936b64/

www.ingramcontent.com/pod-product-compliance
Lightning Source LLC
Chambersburg PA
CBHW020240130626
46549CB00005B/1993